Life at a Public Aquarium

True Animal Stories, Book 2

Life at a Public Aquarium

True Animal Stories, Book 2

By

John Benjamin Sciarra

Acknowledgments

I would like to thank the following people:

Keith M. Cowley, Curator, Living Sharks Museum, Westerly, R.I., USA and the excellent work he is doing in bringing attention to the conservation of sharks. An exceptional artist and scientific illustrator, Keith contributed the mako drawing in the Natural History section. He is also a talented musician and naturalist as well as a paleontologist!

Pamela Sciarra: my wife and fellow Aquarist whose dedication to animals is unparalleled as well as her compassion and love for the ocean, our God, and me (not necessarily in that order).

I would also like to thank the following individuals for setting aside their time to proofread the manuscript and offer creative input: **Pamela Sciarra**: you always have been my most reliable critic as you are well read and intimately familiar with the animals and institution as well as one of my most reliable employees when I was the Curator of Exhibits. **Allison Albert**: you were also an employee at the Aquarium and a smart, knowledgeable and dedicated aquarist and zebrafish expert at Pfizer although you were rarely acknowledged for your contributions. Your familiarity with the natural environment, animals, and history, as well as many subjects, belie your young age. Thank you for your advice and keen eyes. **Amy Kolb**: you brought your expertise in science and zebrafish as well as your experiences at the Aquarium and Pfizer's zebrafish program (now zebrafish specialist at Boston Children's Hospital, Massachusetts). I appreciated the time you spent on this manuscript and the many suggestions that, I hope, will make this publication of interest to all people who might never get the chance to work closely with the magnificent creatures in this world. I know you all share my passion and concern for this beautiful planet and all the life on it.

Aquarists and conservationists everywhere: I know from personal experience that the vast majority of you take what you do seriously and are dedicated to providing the animals in your care with the greatest love and protection, sometimes, as in my case (not always wisely) to our own peril.

Other Books by Author

- Noah's Diary
- Beachmaster
- Shoestrings—No Time For Dinosaurs, Vol 1
- Shoestrings—Paradox, Vol 2
- Shoestrings—Monster In The Lake, Vol 3
- Shoestrings—Echoes Of Time, Vol 4
- No Time For Dinosaurs—**The Novel**
- The Most Tragic Love Story Ever Told
- The Genius Virus
- Samson The Steller Sea Lion, True Animal Stories, Book I

- And several published short stories, including two award winners.

All available on Amazon and online bookstores everywhere.

Introduction

A public aquarium is coming to town! I guess I had been living in a fishbowl my whole life. I didn't know what a public aquarium was. I had never been to one growing up. Our family didn't get out much. The closest thing to a zoo I ever saw was a place called Bates Woods, a small zoo that opened in 1960 in New London, Connecticut. It was within walking distance of my home.

That zoo was where I developed my love for animals, as insignificant as it was compared to just about any other zoo. It had a "Monkey House." The star attraction was a chimpanzee named Rocky. Rocky was kept in a small enclosure resembling a prison with thick bars and only the zoo's keeper and founder, Herbert Moran, would enter (later they named the zoo after Mr. Moran). As Rocky got older, he almost killed Herbert. I don't know what set him off, but it highlights the danger of wild animals in zoos. If I remember correctly, they put Rocky down. I don't think Mr. Moran was ever the same. He was badly injured.

There were smaller monkeys in the enclosure as well. One little guy seemed to revel in luring unsuspecting visitors over to his cage, reaching into their shirt pocket and then peeing in it. The monkey thought that was hysterical. Another one liked to throw feces. I quickly learned to stay far away from him. There were squirrel monkeys that I learned much later could carry potentially deadly diseases as well as capuchins and an assortment of other small primates. My wife, Pamela, worked with capuchins training them to assist handicapped people, but that's a story for a future "True Animal Stories!"

The zoo also housed a variety of other animals such as wolves, llamas, sheep, African lions, mountain lions, bobcats, skunks, raccoons, bears, and beavers, to name a few of what I remember. The zoo was closed after receiving several weighty fines for improper care. Since I had a background in exhibit design, later, while employed at the Mystic Marinelife Aquarium (now the Mystic Aquarium), I offered to help at no cost but was ignored. Guess being a native New Londoner had no pull with the zoo's administrators. I was willing to cover the cost of construction to bring the enclosures up to a minimal standard with natural looking habitats. The one thing they didn't have were fish. No worry; the ocean was nearby.

I loved to fish since I lived so near the ocean. A friend from school lived nearby named Nick, and he taught me how to fish for all manner of fish that inhabited the mouth of the Thames River. I was about ten the first time we went to the State Pier. The water was deep at the end of the dock as large container ships and, occasionally, submarines docked there. We used relatively heavy lead sinkers to get the worms down to the bottom where the flounder dwelt. The area was also densely populated with a fish called the cunner (*Tautogolabrus* *sp.*), a  scavenger. The cunner was a voracious, indiscriminate, eater, while the more reserved flounder seemed to examine the bait suspiciously before biting the succulent earthworms Nick and I had foraged at dusk the night before.

That first time was incredibly exciting to me—even though all we caught were cunner. I was so proud, I brought them home to my father who filleted the dozen or so fish and cooked them over our outside fireplace. They smelled delicious. However, when we tried to eat them, the tiny bones outnumbered flesh. And they tasted even worse. Never again did I bring cunner home for dinner.

Later excursions did produce the much-sought-after flounder (*Psuedoamericanus sp*), a fish well worth the trouble

of catching despite losing a plethora of earthworms to hungry cunner. We did discover that the flounder would strike immediately at the marine sandworm (*Alitta virens*), a scary little creature with vicious-looking pinchers that emerge from its inturned mouth. We cut off the head, more for our own protection, but the juices from that wound

drove the flounder crazy. When they struck the line, it was like an electric shock. We *knew* when it was a flounder and not a cunner. The pole bent down sharply, and we responded by yanking back to set the hook in its mouth.

The experience I acquired during those early years of fishing came in handy whenever I had to collect specimens for the aquarium. One adjustment I made challenged my skills: I used barbless hooks to prevent damage to the fish. In transport and in the aquarium, the chances of infection are significantly increased. I wore plastic gloves and minimized trauma wherever possible.

Much of my early experiences with animals came from my time in the United States Air Force. I was stationed at Loring Air Force Base in Limestone, Maine, where there was little to do unless you were into snow sports. It snowed. A LOT. And the temperatures in the winter could cause frostbite in seconds. Anyway, I had a damaged knee, so I stayed away from skiing and couldn't afford a snowmobile. My wife at the time and I had an extensive collection of animals and fish in our small apartment. One inspector freaked out and told the Base Commander we had a zoo in our house. I had connections, so no one bothered us as long as we weren't rearing poisonous snakes (our boa constrictor simply crushed his dinner. No poison needed!).

We had iguanas, snakes, guinea pigs, rabbits, rats, mice, hamsters, gerbils, and snakes, to name a few. And, of course, a dog. Somewhere along the line we even added a human, our daughter, Lelah who turned out to be quite the animal husbandry expert in her own right and worked in the pet industry (and as an lab animal technician for the University of Rhode Island) for many years even after her mom, Carol, and I went separate ways.

After leaving the Air Force, I was determined to open a full-line pet store. I was told by industry "experts" that no one does that anymore. It would be best to open an aquarium store and, depending on how things went, then add the other animals. I should have listened.

Although Carol and I both had experience with the animals, we weren't adequately prepared for the day-to-day operation of the store despite reading everything we could on retail management. Consequently, while we had the healthiest pets around, we struggled with the costs of running the store. We made mistakes. We might have survived had there not been a second, larger pet store opening just a few miles away — and one with considerably more buying power than us. Also in the competition was a large department store that could purchase pet supplies at a fraction of the cost for either of our smaller stores. In time, both stores failed.

We were forced to move our store, called "Your Local Pet Shoppe," several miles from our location. The landlord sold the land out from under us to a MacDonald's chain and forced us out. The landlord had tried unsuccessfully to burn our store down, have us closed by the Health Department for having rodents and dangerous animals (snakes), and several other nefarious tactics to get us to move. His problem was the lease we signed gave us the option for five years, and that could have killed his deal. After the fire and an invasion of wild rats from the neighboring house, also owned by our landlord, we conceded and moved the store after he agreed to pay for the move. The problem? Our customer base didn't follow to the less convenient location. So, we accepted defeat and closed the store. However, it was at that time that the Aquarium began building its walls, and they were looking for experienced fish people.

One day the newly hired Curator of the Mystic Marinelife Aquarium stopped by our pet store and was impressed with the way we decorated our aquariums and reptile cages. He was also a herp (herpetologist) hobbyist, and we hit it off. He asked if I was interested in working for the Aquarium in building the exhibits. Things weren't going very well with the store, so I agreed to check it out.

The Aquarium rented a small hotel known as Taber Lodge in Mystic, Connecticut, and it had a large building in the back with plenty of wide-open space, cement floors, heat, and ventilation. An exhibit design and construction company owned and operated by Jerry Johnson had the contract for building the exhibits. One of Jerry's designs was the World of Birds at the world-renowned Bronx Zoo in New York. Jerry used fiberglass, cement, and other construction techniques and adapted them to recreate a natural-looking environment for the animals at the zoo.

Along with the Aquarium's Vice President, who had adapted some of those techniques to aquariums, Jerry, Art (one of Jerry's employees), Chris and I were hired to build the interior habitats for all of the aquariums. Later a young lady with extraordinary artistic skills joined us by the name of Sherry.

Fiberglass, when it is curing, has a horrendous, toxic odor. To add to the danger was a thickener known as Aerosil, a silica-based powder that is almost lighter than air. It got airborne when stirred into the fiberglass resin that was pigmented to whatever surface we were building. Our masks were supposed to prevent the toxic fumes from getting into our lungs, but, in retrospect, I think we were lax and the masks wholly inadequate to the task. There were days when I was so dizzy I had to go outside for fresh air. Occasionally, the resin got so hot in the bucket that, if we didn't apply it fast enough, a thick smoke emerged with an even stronger odor. The buckets crackled and popped like a volcano. We ran them outside as soon as that started to happen.

In time, we all became adept at sculpting fiberglass into mud, rocks, and coral. Some of the more delicate structures were cast from latex molds and attached to the base structures of the exhibits. A show on TV nowadays demonstrates how far these techniques have progressed, but we were way ahead of the other aquariums because of Jerry's experience — and some quick learners.

Years later, Jerry and I worked together to create some spectacular coral reefs using techniques and formulas I developed. I wanted to get away from casting corals for two reasons. One, I didn't like using the skeletons of real coral to make molds and, two, I felt the molded corals limited the naturalness and artistic expression of the design. I had seen other exhibits where the corals looked fake. I wanted to fool the observer—and the aquarium's inhabitants, to elicit natural behaviors. Fish bred and fought, darting in and out of the deep nooks and crannies we built into the exhibits as they would in a real reef. We even had one species of fish, the parrotfish, so convinced the coral was real, they started to eat it! I concocted a few fake corals out of Plaster-of-Paris, a calcium-based cement infused with plant material that was edible to give them an option. Mostly it worked. The fish never died anyway, so I guess it was successful. Below is a clipping from The New London Day paper of me fabricating elkhorn coral made by hand. Below that is the completed reef.

Making of a reef — John Sciarra uses nylon string to hold an elk horn coral piece in place until fiberglass hardens as he constructs a new reef exhibit at the Mystic Marinelife Aquarium. The project is expected to be completed Feb. 1 and will feature 50 different kinds of coral, including brain, elk horn, and stag horn corals, and at least 15 varieties of Caribbean fish species. The fiberglass construction weighs about 900 pounds and will be housed in a new tank that holds 7,500 gallons of water. Sciarra has the assistance of four volunteers.

During construction, I was sent to the Aquarium of Niagara Falls, our sister Aquarium owned by the same company, to learn from their seasoned and professional aquarists. Many of the exhibits were built by our VP when he worked there years earlier. The sudden immersion into the world of the aquarist was exhilarating. I was enthralled with the variety of animals in simulated habitats made of artificial materials, including the fiberglass corals and rockwork techniques I had acquired.

Also, I watched the dolphins, seals and sea lions demonstrate a variety of learned behaviors up close. I absorbed every detail of the training in the two to three weeks I was there. When I returned to Mystic, I was ready to plunge into my assignment as the first aquarist. Much of what I learned came by hard-learned lessons and the expert guidance of our VP whose experience was world-renown. It was a fortunate happenstance for me. That, and a voracious appetite to learn everything and anything I could about the animals and their environments. There was just so much to learn!

After many months, the exhibits were built, and the Aquarium was coming together. Glass was installed, filters and gravel were added, and the artificial saltwater added. More about opening day at a later time. First, let me tell you about some of the fantastic animals and opportunities I had working at what I thought was the greatest job in the world!

One of my later projects with all hand-sculpted corals constructed out of fiberglass and epoxy.

Chapter One

SEA LIONS

So, you've been to a public aquarium. Maybe you made funny noises at the sea lions and seals, but they ignored you. Perhaps you weren't speaking their language. Then, you watched a show. Dolphins jumped through hoops and walked on their tail flukes. Maybe a sea lion impressed you by standing on one flipper while holding a beach ball on his nose and caught rings thrown from a trainer, all at the same time! Then the trainer came up and patted the sea lion on the back while feeding him or her pieces of fish. So cute! You're thinking, "I'd like to take him home." Well, I have a surprise for you. Sea lions — all sea lions — are not anywhere near as affectionate as you might think.

The California Sea Lion (*Zalophus californianus*), for example, tolerates being touched and patted because of intensive behavioral conditioning through numerous training sessions often over the years. Allowing humans to touch them it is not a natural activity like it is for a dog or cat. If this training takes place when the animal is relatively young, touching is tolerated and gives viewers the impression that the animal is affectionate. Such is rarely the case, as the following story would seem to indicate.

The Aquarium staff had been invited to appear on a local television talk show. One of our trainers, Cindy, was working with a young California Sea Lion named Squirty. Cindy, had complete control over Squirty even under the studio conditions with bright lights and cameras — until the show host decided to come up to Squirty without warning to "pet" him! The horrified trainer tried to stop him, but she didn't react quickly enough.

Squirty turned in an instant and roared at the host and snapped with his sharp teeth. Even a young sea lion can exert several thousand pounds of pressure per square inch with those jaws. Fortunately for the television host, Squirty missed. The host jumped back, visibly shaken and tried to regain his composure. After all, the cameras were still rolling. Squirty instantly returned to the commands of the trainer as if nothing had happened at all. There was no hatred in his reaction. He was simply responding to what he thought was a threat.

I was off camera not far from Squirty holding a small harbor seal (*Phoca vitulina*) named Rocky. Rocky was the first marine mammal I ever laid eyes on up close. I remember how frightened I had been of him when he was only a pup weighing around thirty pounds. He growled at me the first time I tried to hold him, and I jumped back like a frightened little kid. My supervisor stood *outside* the enclosure and made fun of me.

"What'ya scared? Come on. He's just a *baby!*"

I invited my supervisor to demonstrate, and he declined. Big surprise. He had never handled a harbor seal either. The course of wisdom when handling unfamiliar animals is not to play "*Crocodile Hunter.*" You're more likely to keep all of your fingers if you're at least a *little* frightened. As I learned how animals reacted in any given circumstance, I became more adept at handling them. I was doing okay with Rocky that day in the television studio—until Squirty noticed he had company!

Squirty, his attention turned from the control of the trainer, spotted Rocky and decided to jump off his seat and give chase. I don't know if it was aggression or that Squirty just wanted to play, but Rocky wasn't hanging around to find out. He broke free from my grasp. Harbor seals tend to move like an inchworm by undulating their bodies, unlike the sea lion whose hinged hips allow them to scamper pretty fast on land. Rocky undulated rather quickly, though, through the studio—under lights, TV cameras, and cameramen who scurried to get out of the way. Our veterinarian was howling hysterically with laughter despite the frantic cries of the host who was desperately trying to regain control of his show. It's a shame the cameramen couldn't have got all of this on camera, but they were too busy running for their lives.

We grabbed a large board and managed to steer Squirty into a back room next to the studio. Unfortunately, there was a group of clowns from the local police department waiting to go on. I mean no offense to the police department here. They really were dressed in clown suits! One of the officers had a large, dead, codfish in his hands—I don't know why, but this isn't a particularly good thing to have in your possession in the presence of a hungry sea lion running rampant around the place unless you're the trainer.

When they caught sight of Squirty heading in their direction growling and barking, the cod went flying, and the clowns bolted, terrified out of their wits. They managed to escape. It may not have been part of their act, but I had tears streaming down my face from laughing so hard.

Our company vehicle, a green Chevy Suburban, was parked just inside a garage door. We decide to corral Squirty into the back of the Suburban and figure out what to do from there. Squirty only weighed about one hundred and twenty pounds, but the bite of even a small sea lion can be serious.

After an hour of being chased around, Squirty became tired and jumped into the back of the truck, but not before knocking a small glass aquarium out of the back causing it to shatter into a million pieces of sharp shards and splinters. Fortunately, Squirty's cage was in the back of the truck already, and he was only too happy, at this point, to retire to the relative peace and quiet of it. I just closed the cage door, and he took a nap.

Unfortunately, the best part of the chase wasn't on film, but you get some idea of how quickly a situation can get out of control. In fact, that same trainer was grabbed on stage in front of an audience by a much larger sea lion named Salty—a veteran performer with no history of aggression. Her collarbone was dislocated when Salty picked her up in his mouth and shook her for no apparent reason. Salty weighed about 450 pounds! It was a frightening experience for the trainer. We retired Salty to our Seal Island exhibit after that incident where I got to work with him. The trainer that was injured decided to retire from working with sea lions altogether.

Wild animals in the hands of a trained handler may appear to be affectionate and docile. Years of training and experience are necessary to work with these animals safely. However, even under the best of circumstances, things don't always go as planned. *Boy, do they ever not go as planned!*

Chapter Two

PIERRE

Pierre was a grey seal (Halichoerus grypus), also known as the horsehead head seal for obvious reasons. Grey seals are quite common in the northern Atlantic. They are similar in appearance to the much smaller harbor seal but are considerably larger. Pierre weighed about 900 pounds. Most of the time, he was extremely quiet and docile. However, I soon found out that, during the breeding season, all the rules changed. When that day came…

Pierre's eyes were glazed over with only one thought on his mind. Nine hundred pounds of prime blubber and a full coat of gray hair, he turned and took in the beauty of his true love. With his heart beating wildly at sixty beats per minute (that's a lot for a seal), nature's instinct of breeding was, at this moment, the most crucial thing in his life. Not the need for food; not the need to migrate; no body function could stop him from his objective: to mate! Only one thing stood between this massive, undulating, mass of quivering blubber, muscle and flesh and the seal of his dreams — *me*.

Pierre was about twenty-five at the time and reasonably docile. One day earlier in the season, we had drained his pool in the New England Coast. The exhibit needed a thorough cleaning. Algae was discoloring the bottom of the pool. Several of the young harbor seals were sliding across the pool bottom and splashing through the stream of water shooting from the end of the hose as I cleaned the bottom. They're a riot to watch as they fly across the slick pool bottom obviously enjoying themselves immensely. The spray from the garden hose was causing a mist to form over the pool, and a rainbow would appear and arch across the pool as steam rose from the backs of the seals. I was having so much fun watching them, I decided to sit down on the only available seat in the pool: Pierre's back.

Pierre casually looked over his shoulder at me briefly and then resumed his nap without a care in the world. At that moment, the vice president of the Aquarium came out onto the beach and began chuckling to himself.

"What's so funny?" I asked.

He replied, "Let me tell you something about that *dangerous* animal you're sitting on so calmly."

"Pierre? Dangerous?"

"Yes! When I worked at the New York Aquarium some years back, *three people* were required to be present in the pool whenever it was drained and cleaned — like you're doing here. We were in a union then. The union said that *two* people were needed to hold a large, heavy board against Pierre to *protect* the other person who was hosing off the pool bottom. They were *terrified* of him! I just wanted you to know how much danger you're in at this very moment."

I looked over at Pierre. He opened one eye and snorted. A bit of mucous blew out his nostrils (which is quite common among seals and sea lions). I began laughing, hysterically. Pierre remained indifferent. He was indeed a docile animal.

Another animal in our collection of New England seals was Selchie, a female grey seal. She, too, had come to us from New York. Considerably older than Pierre, Selchie was totally blind. Her eyes had turned white with cataracts from old age and intense sunlight. Although our exhibit in Mystic was designed to provide areas of refuge from the sun with broad, overhanging evergreens, it was too late to be of any benefit to Selchie.

At night and early in the morning, Selchie's plaintive cry could be heard echoing across the small manmade lake that used to span the area between the main Aquarium building and Seal Island. Selchie wasn't sad — she just sounded that way. It was her way of communicating although I really can't say with any certainty what it was she wanted. However, during the breeding season, it took on a sense of urgency.

Selchie wasn't the prettiest grey seal on earth by a long shot. In fact, she had the disgusting habit of shredding the mackerel I fed her into strips of bloody flesh and bones. Most every other self-respecting seal or sea lion (except for a rather pugnacious female elephant seal named Grumble) would swallow their fish whole without the mess. When Selchie was finished eating, her face was covered with blood and mucus, which dripped off her chin and down onto her chest. The shorter pectoral flippers had long claws on them, unlike the sea lions whose longer flippers had much shorter ones. It was this feature that allowed Selchie to make such a mess. She would take the whole fish from me by extending her vibrissae—long sensitive whiskers on each side of her face—and then begin the slaughter. Her mouth always smelled like—dead fish!

None of this seemed to deter the love-struck Pierre. That cold, fall day, I stood there for a moment between Pierre and Selchie and was about to begin feeding the animals in the exhibit. As Pierre moved in my direction with a very determined look, I assumed he was just hungry. Here I was standing there in my parka, jeans and rubber boots with two large buckets of fish for the dozen or so harbor seals and several grey seals that were waiting anxiously for their morning meal. I noticed that there was a distant look in Pierre's eyes. It was as if he didn't even see me. I felt as if he were looking right through me!

I shouted his name, but he just kept coming. I jumped out of the way at the last second when I realized he wasn't going to stop. In the process, I dropped the stainless-steel buckets of fish, and he ran over them, flattening them like pancakes along with the fish. It was a moment before I realized what was going on. Pierre headed right for Selchie, who rejected his advances with loud screams. She scurried off into the water spooking all of the other animals in the pool.

Pierre's intentions were never to hurt me. He was just following his instincts. If there is a moral to this experience, I would guess it would be: Never stand in the way of true love—especially when it is between a half ton suitor and the object of his affection.

Chapter Three

BAD IDEAS

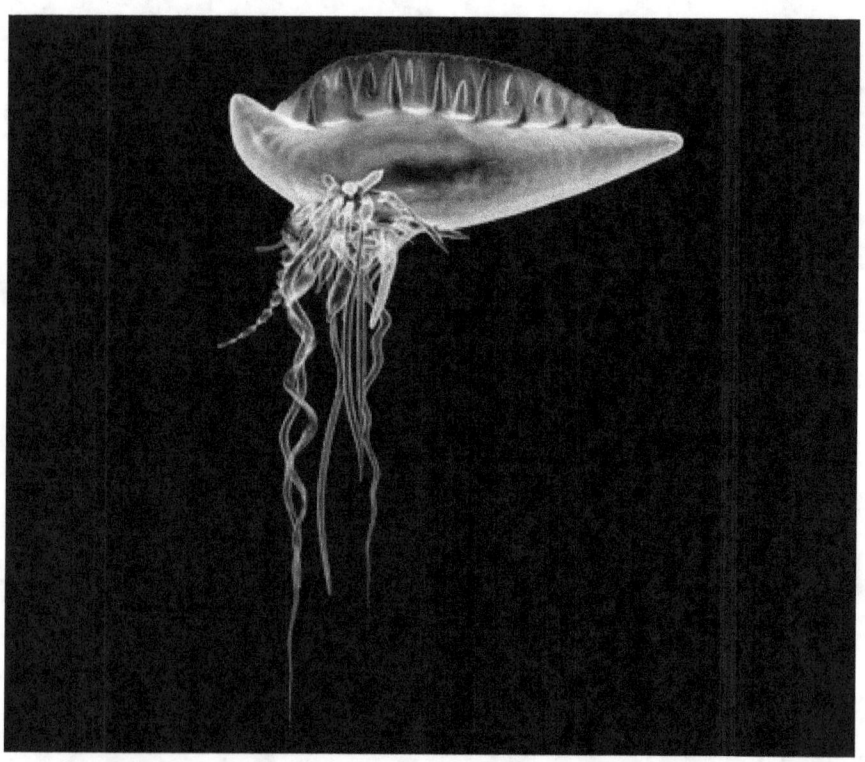

Working with wild animals in captivity, as indicated above, obviously *can be dangerous*. Zoo workers have been injured or killed working with elephants, alligators, crocodiles, poisonous snakes, sharks—and sea lions. More often than not, the handler not being able to anticipate the actions of the animal causes the mistake. Sometimes, however, it's just plain stupidity, as the following experiences would seem to indicate.

One of our *aquarists* (what animal handlers at a public aquarium are called) was fascinated with the arrival of an unexpected guest. A local fisherman had brought in an unusual jellyfish he had scooped up in a bucket while fishing off Block Island, New York. It was a "man-o-war" capable of inflicting a painful sting to the unwary diver or swimmer.

Usually, these animals are found in much warmer waters, but all manner of tropical animals find their way into the New England waters at the end of summer on eddies spun off from the Gulf Stream. The Gulf Stream is a current of warm water that snakes like a river up the coast frequently coming close enough to send New England the tropical visitors. I've caught butterflyfish, parrotfish, angelfish, and other tropical fish while diving off of Jamestown, Rhode Island. But the man-o-war was quite a surprise.

I watched James as he stood there, staring in fascination at the inflated air sac sticking up out of the water like a balloon. It was purplish-black with a little red and blue—a sure sign to predators that it was poisonous. The air sac helps to propel the man-o-war through the water, allowing it to trap small fish and other creatures in its long, thin tentacles. The tentacles can reach over 30 feet in length!

Ours was just a baby. It fit into a thirty-gallon aquarium. I didn't think much about James when he kept going back and forth to the man-o-war all day long. I warned him not to touch the tentacles, but even adults sometimes let their curiosity get the better of them.

The following morning, I got a phone call from James. He wouldn't be in to work because he was up all night.

"Why?" I asked. There was a hesitation on the line. James really didn't want to tell me.

"Well, ...you know that man-o-war?"

"Yeah..."

"Well...I touched the tentacle, and nothing happened. So, I took a little *tiny* piece of the tentacle...and put it on my finger."

"Yeah..."

"And...I guess I forgot about it."

"You *left* it on your finger?"

"Yeah."

"*All* day?"

"Uh...yeah. It didn't hurt."

"And..."

"Well, now my finger is twice its normal size. It's really, really red and it won't stop throbbing. I couldn't sleep, it hurt so bad."

"Maybe you should call the doctor. Or you could wait until it falls off."

"Okay, I'll call the doctor."

James' finger returned to normal size—a week later. I think he learned his lesson.

Chapter Four

DEATH OF THE LIONFISH

The main exhibit area of the Aquarium was dark when I arrived, as I usually did six-days-a-week, at 6:00 AM. I was always the first one there. As Lead Aquarist, it was my job to turn on the first stage of overhead lighting in the exhibits to avoid *photoshock* in the tanks' inhabitants. Suddenly turning on all of the lights at once can wreak havoc with the immune systems of the fish and lead to disease outbreaks. This was my favorite time of the day.

Usually. I had the whole place to myself. Well, me and about a thousand other creatures.

While the animals were adjusting for the next thirty minutes or so until I turned on the rest of the lights, I busied myself with pulling the partially-thawed fish foods to prepare for the day's feedings. There were a variety of animals to feed, including sharks and other fishes, invertebrates, crustaceans, as well as the marine mammals ranging from seals and sea lions to whales and dolphins. The whales and dolphins responsibility belonged to the trainers. The sand tiger sharks looked menacing as they swam through the shadows of the 30,000-gallon Open Ocean exhibit. Really, they were harmless despite the sharp teeth sticking out of their mouths. I frequently dove in the tank to clean the bottom filter. The sharks were more afraid of me than I of them.

Once the lighting was at full capacity, I grabbed my "Daily Check List" and made my rounds recording the water chemistry and temperature for each exhibit, replacing burned out bulbs and checking the condition of the animals and exhibit presentation. There were two separate alcoves in our main exhibit area: "Communities" and "Adaptations." The Community exhibits were slices of ocean habitats such as "Offshore Waters," and "Atlantic Coral Reef," among others. The Adaptations Alcove housed mostly smaller aquariums, around 200 gallons, and served to educate our visitors about the variety of specialized abilities of a variety of species.

Having performed this routine for several years, it was almost second nature. I could spot a problem from across one alcove to the other in the blink of an eye. If anything was out-of-whack, I knew it. This morning, I stopped in my tracks. It didn't take an expert to spot it. An entire tankful of fish was floating belly-up.

It might sound strange, but I expected this would happen. Nevertheless, it was a shock. Unfortunately, it was a common occurrence in the world of professional aquarists with this particular species of fish—and it was an enigma. No one seemed to know why it happened all of a sudden like that or what to do about it. For myself, I *never* accepted ignorance as an excuse, though I possessed an ample amount of it. Where I had a gap in knowledge, and believe me there were plenty of those, I made it my mission to fill the void whenever I could. One excuse that still drives me crazy is, "Well, that's always the way we did it."

The fish that were currently floating were called lionfish of the species *Pterois volitans*. These are extraordinarily beautiful, colorful fish with elegant, long and delicate-looking dancing fins with black stripes intermixed with orange and red. Most notable are the long spines cascading across the back or dorsal side of the fish. Despite the attractiveness, those spines contained a potent toxin, and the colors, a warning to all predators to stay far away. The lionfish is also a voracious predator in its own right. The spines were for defense, but it could swallow any fish it could get into its mouth whole in a flash of movement. It was the lionfish's appetite that got it into trouble as you'll see in a moment.

The very first time I laid eyes on a lionfish was at the Aquarium of Niagara Falls in New York. I was awestruck by their beauty. They looked healthy, bigger than I expected, and quite fat. I was at the Aquarium as part of my training as an Assistant Aquarist. There was no "Aquarist" yet, and I found that peculiar, but you have to start somewhere in the business, and that was my title despite being the *only* aquarist.

I was told by my trainer that the lionfish only ate live food and the food of choice, for economic and accessibility reasons, was the common goldfish. Once a day, a net full of goldfish was dumped into the aquarium for the anxious carnivores. They devoured their meals in a matter of seconds. It was astonishing to watch. I learned that the lifespan of the lionfish was less than two years. Most curious was that they all died on the same day. No one seemed to know why. I stored that tidbit of information for future reference. That day, it came in handy. At least I was expecting it!

Mystic had its own lionfish exhibit in our "Adaptations" alcove demonstrating the defensive adaptation of their venomous spines along the dorsal fin, which only added to the elegance of this beautiful creature. We too, as I had been taught, fed the lionfish with goldfish.

These voracious eaters seem to have no concept of how many goldfish they could physically get into their stomachs. Often, I saw the tail of an unfortunate food fish sticking out of the mouth of a bloated lionfish still moving; the belly of the perpetually hungry predator was extended like a puffer fish fully inflated. Our fish looked healthy — on the outside. However, like those at Niagara Falls, they all met the same fate less than a year later. I found them all floating in the somewhat frothy water. Even though I expected it might happen, it was still disturbing to witness a mass death like that. No one with any measure of empathy for animals can completely block out the loss of any of the creatures under his or her care. I felt a sense of loss. And failure.

I netted out all of the specimens and took them to our laboratory. Then I drained the aquarium and turned off the lights. I would have to sanitize the tank, set it back up and order more fish. It would take more than a month to get the exhibit opened again. In the meantime, as was my routine, I necropsied all of the fish and discovered something surprising. All of their livers were discolored. Some were yellow; others had a sickly-looking white blotchy appearance. Healthy looking livers were dark, reddish brown. I took samples of the organs, and our lab tech ran histology slides to determine the condition of the livers microscopically. As I suspected, there were fatty deposits permeating the tissues at the cellular level. Despite their apparently healthy looking exterior, something was going on internally. How could this be, I wondered; when the fish were well fed and looked so good? And why on earth would they *all* die at once on the same night? I had a theory, and an idea popped into my mind on how to test at least the sudden death syndrome. The fatty livers were still another problem, but I would come across a clue thanks to a wounded snowy egret and a friend who was a veterinarian.

My hypothesis about the sudden death was just a logical conclusion. I thought, what if *one* of the fish died because of the liver disease, whatever that was, and, at death, it released its poison from the glands at the base of its spines? I came up with a way to test my theory, but it would take another year to prove.

If my theory was correct, I thought I could prevent all of the fish from dying by installing a carbon filter on the filter system. An added feature of the carbon was spectacularly crystal-clear water. Typically, we employed a sub-gravel biological filter that effectively removes the wastes from the fish. All of our systems operated the same way. It is a process known as nitrification and is a natural process in nature. However, the carbon can *adsorb* (to chemically remove particles by ion attraction rather than *absorb,* which is a mechanical method such as in a sponge) other waste products not removed by the filter. In doing so, it clarifies the water and, I hoped, would trap the toxins released from the first lionfish to succumb to the liver disease. Time would tell, as they say.

A little over a year later, sure enough, we lost one fish. However, all of the others were fine. I immediately replaced the carbon in the filter, as the adsorptive ability has its limits when all of the ions have filled the surfaces of the carbon. So far, it seemed, my theory was panning out.

I necropsied the deceased animal and, sure enough, it had the same liver condition of the previous animals. That also meant that, eventually, we would lose all of the others. In time, they all died, too. But there was no mass die off, and we didn't need to break the tank down and start over again thanks to the carbon filter system. Still, there was the root cause of the problem. *Why* were the lionfish getting fatty livers? I wondered; are the goldfish the problem? If you pay attention to all of the little things going on around you and store that information for later use, it's incredible to me how solutions appear from the most unexpected places.

A good friend of mine from years earlier when I owned and operated a pet store with my family had the unusual habit of rescuing all manner of animals. I never knew what strange creature would show up in his house. One day there was a barn owl under the sink in his bathroom. In the living room, a large tank housed a reticulated python some ten feet in length that outgrew its owner's ability to care for it. He and I had opened a hospital of sorts for reptiles in the back of our family's pet store—the only one in the state of Connecticut at the time. Dr. Rob's abilities extended beyond his medical expertise as well. He was an extraordinary cabinet maker and built me several reptile enclosures for our hospital/serpentarium that attracted visitors just to see the collection of snakes, lizards, and turtles. Maybe if we had charged admission, I would have stayed in business!

One day while visiting Dr. Rob and his wife, I was surprised to see a full-grown bittern (a shorebird) walking around his living room. Dr. Rob had repaired a broken wing, but he was having trouble feeding it. His food source was none other than that of our lionfish: goldfish — *lots* of them. But the bird was losing weight despite eating almost constantly. The bird died, and we were puzzled. It was about the same time that I was contemplating the mystery of the lionfish. I wondered if there was a connection. Then I found it — again from another unexpected source — seals and sea lions!

It was well-established that the food fishes that were fed to seals and sea lions in captivity contained an enzyme that destroyed a vital vitamin, vitamin B-1 or thiamine. The problem was made worse when frozen fish, the primary source of the marine mammals' food, had a higher amount of the enzyme, thiaminase which breaks down thiamine, due to a process known as *autolysis*. Under natural conditions, this isn't a problem. However, in captivity, it was necessary to supplement the food for the marine mammals with a vitamin B-1 tablet. I knew this since a facet of my job included the care of our seal and sea lion population in our "Seal Island" exhibit that housed a variety of marine mammals. Every day before opening the exhibit, we gave all of the mammals a single fish with a B-1 and a vitamin tablet to prevent a deficiency that could result in the death of the animals. I wondered if there might be a connection. But, we fed *live* fish. How could a thiamine deficiency be the cause of the liver problem in lionfish? I thought it was worth investigating.

I did a lot of reading on fish nutrition. In fact, it became a pet project. There were still many unknowns and — even today — there are still many holes in the knowledge of fish nutrition. Research is always ongoing. There are just so many different species of fish with staggering differences of food sources even in nature, sometimes making it difficult, or even impossible to duplicate a specific species' natural foods. Often, our approach was called the "shotgun" method. Feed a bunch of different foods and hope that somewhere along the line, you covered all of the nutritional bases.

One night, while reading an article, I discovered a study that indicated high levels of thiaminase in the common goldfish. It was a jaw-drop moment. Could we have been inadvertently killing our lionfish by depriving them of vitamin B-1 by feeding them live goldfish?

In my studies, I discovered a great deal I didn't know about the nutrition of fish. Most of the research papers and books I read were about commercially important fish for human consumption such as the salmon, trout, and catfish raised on fish farms. Commercial fish foods were available for those species, and we fed them to our own trout and other freshwater fish. I was always told that, in no uncertain terms, lionfish would never eat anything but live fish. While we were able to substitute some locally caught fish such as mummichogs, we didn't have it in our budget to feed all of our lionfish other species that were available from the pet industry. Plus, there was always the possibility of introducing disease. Fortunately, my research into the nutritional requirements of fish led me down another path that would, eventually, benefit the lionfish a well as a host of other marine fish. Jell-O!

I had an occasion one day to visit the magnificent New England Aquarium in Boston, Massachusetts. Situated near the mouth of the Boston Harbor, it dwarfs the smaller Mystic Aquarium in size, scope and animal population. The day I was there, I noticed an animal handler feeding a sea lion something strange. I asked what it was. "Gelatin diet" was the response. I was dumbstruck. "Why on earth would you feed sea lions Jell-O?" "Not 'Jell-O,' *gelatin*. It's unflavored, and we use it to bind special diets for some of our animals with special needs, nutritionally."

At first, I was puzzled. But I was intrigued. Our VP directed me to an article that had been written about a gelatin diet for trout, and I took a trip to the Woods Hole Oceanographic Institute's library in Massachusetts and found the paper. I made a copy. Since I was attending night school at a local college, I inquired if I might conduct an independent study to see if I could come up with a gelatin-based diet for marine fish. The idea was approved, and I set about duplicating the diet which had, at the root of its formula, trout meal. The diet was reasonably sound as far as I could determine based on all the available nutritional data for trout and our trout ate it well enough. But, apparently, marine fishes are much more discriminating in taste. No matter how I sliced it, literally, they ignored the gelatin, and I had to scoop it out of all the aquariums when it dropped to the bottom. I wondered if it was a matter of taste—again, literally.

I decided to approach the problem from a completely different perspective much to chagrin of our Curator who made fun of me for not following the "scientific method." I convinced him to be patient. This, I told him, was a question of first, finding out whether I could flavor the gelatin to the liking of the fish. Once I accomplished that, I could then adjust the nutritional value which, I suspected, might be different for different species.

To make a long story short, in time I discovered the taste preferences of all of the marine fish and designed three recipes based on the basic three categories of diet: Herbivorous (plant-based), carnivorous (primarily flesh eaters) and omnivorous (a little bit of each). I wrote and published several papers on the diet and gained a bit of notoriety and a measly single credit from the college course. Next, I faced what could have been my biggest challenge: lionfish. To say I faced a bit of ridicule for my idea that I could get the lionfish to eat a gelatin diet was putting it mildly.

We were still experiencing the fatty livers and ultimate death at around two years, although I had solved the issue of the sudden death of the whole school with the carbon filtration. I felt something was amiss in the dietary requirements of the fish. I had a new theory. Our lionfish were eating too much, too fast, and the diet was overly rich in fatty acids. I decided I was going to train the lionfish using the same techniques as any animal: behavioral modification.

I postulated that I could start each feeding with a signal to pre-condition the fish to expect the food. While just showing up was usually enough, I wanted to signal something different. It was simple, a few taps on the edge of the tank. We did this for the first week before feeding the live fish to them. Next, I fed strips of smelt, a low-oil fish after tapping. The lionfish went after the strips in much the same manner as the live food. I did this for another week.

The third week I made the strips of fish chunkier. Same response. I did this for another week. Then, I dropped in the gelatin diet I used for the carnivores, which had a balance of vitamins and lower density of fatty acids and high protein content. It worked! I not only proved that lionfish could be trained to eat dead fish, but they could be trained to eat the gelatin diet as well.

At this point, I had been promoted to Assistant Curator and had a little more authority. I directed our aquarists to feed the lionfish specific amounts of gelatin every other day. The fish grew much more slowly, but they were healthy looking. Two years later, they were all still alive. Three, four, and five years later, they were still with us. By this time, we had begun feeding each fish on a pole to ensure all got the same amount. Not only was the mystery of the lionfish mass deaths solved, but we had proven beyond a doubt that lionfish could live for more than two years.

The program worked so well, I adapted it to a tank full of exotic moral eels also reported to only eat live food. Now, if only I could get my daughter to eat provolone cheese.

While still on the subject of the lionfish, I have to relate a somewhat amusing incident. I received a phone call one day from a frantic man. He had a lionfish in an aquarium at his home. As I mentioned, the lionfish has a row of poisonous spines on its dorsal fin. This ribbon-like fin hides a lethal weapon. Inside of each spine is a hollow tube that ends in a sharp needle-like tip. At the base of the spine is the organ that contains poison. Whenever anything comes in contact with the spine, the organ automatically injects any potential predators. It's more of a defensive weapon to keep predators at bay.

Most animals of the oceans, like the man-o-war, have brilliant colors that are a warning to any predators to stay away. Any predator dumb enough to ignore that warning quickly learns they should have dined elsewhere.

When the caller told me he had been accidentally injected in his arm by the lionfish, I became alarmed. "How do you feel?" I asked.

"My arm is twice its normal size."

"Are you having any difficulty breathing?"

"No."

I explained that the poison of the lionfish is not unlike that of a bee sting. In some people, it can cause severe allergic reactions—even death. I gave him the same advice I gave James when he had been stung by the man-o-war.

"I suggest you call a doctor right away." The man's response caught me completely off guard.

"I *am* a doctor. I wanted to know if I should call a priest!"

Chapter 6

SHARKS!

Opening a new public aquarium is a significant undertaking. It involves many people and many, many hours of labor. Frequently, I worked over one hundred hours *per week!* A few times, I went without a day off for three months at a time and even had a few times I didn't sleep for 48 hours straight because I was busy working. However, one of my favorite memories was when I went fishing for sharks for our Open Ocean exhibit off Cape May, New Jersey.

It was 10:00 in the morning and the skies were clear except for an occasional puffy white cloud drifting across the periwinkle-blue expanse. The sun was erupting off of the horizon like a giant red bubble bursting in slow motion. It sent slivers of silver and orange in every direction as it glistened off the putrid waters off Cape May. But just at a glance, one couldn't tell the water was foul. When I reached over the side and scooped up a handful of water, I could see that it was discolored.

A shark fin menacingly broke the water every so often as we cut a path through the mouth of the bay, and this encouraged us. After all, we weren't in danger of sinking, which might have changed our point of view. We were here to bring live sharks back to the brand new Mystic Marinelife Aquarium in Mystic, Connecticut. It was due to open in a few days and, of course, everyone wanted to see "man-eating" sharks.

Our captain told us that the local fishermen had been reporting catches of small — that is to say four or five-foot-long — sand bar, duskies, and an occasional sand tiger. It was the sand tiger in particular we desired. These magnificent creatures have an impressive set of dentures with long sharp teeth sticking out in every which direction which gives them the intimidating look of a man-eater. Only the great white is more frightening in appearance, but with good cause. On the other hand, the sand tiger only *looks* dangerous. We had heard that there were no reported attacks on humans from these animals although I didn't want to volunteer to jump in the water with one to test that theory out.

The water was calm that morning, a good thing since we had driven through the night and only gotten an hour of sleep. The first thing we did was head for the mouth of the bay where the captain had dropped a longline the night before. A longline consists of several hundred feet of strong line with wire leaders and large baited hooks extending out at various depths. It is weighted at the end with a cinder block. If we had caught any sharks on the longline, we could have headed right back to the docks, loaded the truck and driven back to Connecticut. That wouldn't have been much of an adventure, but it would have been efficient. As it turned out, the longline was missing. Either it had been cut and stolen, or it had simply been taken out with the tide. In either case, it looked like we were going to fish with rod and reel. I was excited! I had never caught anything larger than a ten-pound blackfish before, and here I was hunting for one of the largest predators of the sea.

The captain (I think his name was Bill, but for all intents and purposes he could have been Frank Mundus, the inspiration for Quint, the Captain in the movie, Jaws!) had his mates set up the bait, and I was given a deep-sea fishing rod and reel setup. I sat in the chair and waited as the bait drifted away from the boat, and we trolled slowly along. Occasionally, one of the mates would throw a cup full of bloody fish guts overboard. I don't know about the sharks, but it sure didn't do much for my stomach. I was never one given to motion sickness as a rule, but I felt clearly on the brink of changing that aspect of my existence. Joe had a rod and reel setup as well and was seated next to me in an adjoining chair. He looked like I felt. He said, "Well, John, it looks like we're going to get some sharks! Just sit back and let's get some big ones." We were told that as soon as someone had a strike, the other should reel in immediately to prevent entanglement. This was going to be *fun*!

Within ten minutes, I felt the line get *very* heavy. The pole bent down to the deck, and I had to hold on with everything I had. Captain Bill yelled. "Get the other lines in! Quick! Or we'll tangle!" Joe started reeling in like crazy with a loud, high-pitched "zzzzzzzz" sound. My line began to unwind as the drag (a resistance built into the reel assembly to prevent the line from breaking) reached its maximum capacity. I tried lifting the tip of the rod, but it wouldn't budge. I looked over to the Captain questioningly. He growled, "Well? Reel 'em in! What'dya waitin' for? Come on!"

The line just kept splaying out at a rapid pace. I was sure I had accidentally hooked a small submarine. After what seemed like an hour, but in reality, was only a few minutes, the run stopped, and the line went slack. Whatever it was had, let go. I was crushed. I started to reel back in with no tension on the line. I had it almost back to the boat when, without warning, the pole snapped back down to the deck again, nearly pulling me out of the chair. One of the mates strapped me in. I really didn't want to start barefoot water skiing behind a shark or whale or whatever it was at the end of my line. I admit I was a little frightened by whatever it was. If this was a little four or five-foot shark, you could have the big ones. This was out of my league.

The captain was convinced it was small, and he began ridiculing me for not being able to bring the monster in.

"Come on ya little sissy. That all ya got? What a'ya a weakling? We ain't got all day ya know!"

So, I began to tighten down on the drag to increase resistance on the reel. I wasn't going to let this thing get away. Now the captain got *mad* at me for doing this!

"What a' ya doing! Y'er gonna break my reel!"

Some people! How else was I going to bring it in? I was fighting this thing for over forty-five minutes, and still, it would swim toward me and then back out again unraveling all of the line. We finally decided that, in the interest of getting on with the expedition, we should just cut the shark loose. I didn't like that option. My pride was still on the line, and the photographer was still documenting. How would that look in the paper? I wouldn't be able to face my family and friends. Such was the mentality of my young male mind. Beat the killer fish and be a hero.

Finally, the shark became exhausted. I was only a few minutes away from exhaustion myself. My arms hurt, and my hands were sore. As I reeled the spent animal up to the boat, I couldn't believe what I was seeing. It was enormous! The monster was over eight feet long and probably weighed over three hundred pounds. It was a sand tiger, and he was every bit as ferocious looking as the pictures I had seen. My heart was beating wildly in my chest. Never had I been so excited over a fish! I had caught my first real, live shark! What a fabulous addition to the collection this would make.

However, such was not to be the case. The live boxes we had brought with us were only six feet long. While I wasn't a whiz in math, even I could figure this one out. There was simply no way to bring this monster aboard without folding him up like an accordion. The photographer from the Courant got some great shots, and a photo of the creature with his mouth open and all those nasty teeth hanging all over the place made the front page in the weekend section. One other photo showed me lying on top of the bow section sound asleep.

The Captain cut the line, and the old killer went back to his watery home carrying with him a souvenir—the hook—which I was assured would simply fall out after a couple of months. He must have been the envy of all his friends (if sharks have friends) with that ornament.

After a few minutes rest, Joe and I put our lines back in and, as things go, I hooked another shark almost immediately. I wanted to give the rod to Joe, but the crew had already made it clear that I was a wimp. In the interest of preserving my fragile male ego, I accepted the new challenge. This one fought well, but it was clear that it wasn't as big as the eight-footer. After twenty minutes, I landed him. It was a six-foot sandbar shark. A beautiful, sleek animal. We decided to see if it would fit in the box. We had six boxes on board each about six feet long, sitting on the deck equipped with bubblers for the air. A sump pump was used to fill the container quickly.

The captain and his mate dropped a nylon noose over the shark and heaved it aboard. The idea was to drop it directly *into* the box. They missed. Suddenly, the shark came back to life. *Apparently*, they don't like being out of the water. Big surprise there. It went ballistic—writhing and snapping at legs and feet. We had two options as I saw it. Jump in the water or be bitten. Neither option was very appealing since we had been chumming with fish blood and guts and attracted quite a few fins that were now cruising all around the boat. Now, chances are they wouldn't have eaten us, but there was a *strong* possibility they would have at least tried before deciding that we were more toxic than the other creatures they usually eat. Then again, sharks have been found with old car tires, beer cans, and license plates in their stomach. Perhaps we were slightly more digestible. Frenzied sharks have been even known to eat *themselves* in the heat of a feeding frenzy.

The quick thinking (albeit gauche) captain motioned for all of us to get onto the *transom*, which we obeyed without question. Now, to those of you unfamiliar with boats, the transom is that tiny little ledge that runs around the rim of the boat. In this case, it was very thin, perhaps only a few inches wide. It's amazing what you can hold onto when hard-pressed. The captain came to the conclusion the animal wouldn't have been very comfortable in the small box anyway, and he managed to get the shark back in the water. The collection of hooks these guys were sporting was increasing.

Sometime later in the morning, we came alongside another boat loaded with beer-guzzling shark hunters (technically, we had done that the night before so that label might not apply to us). We watched them reel one in with curiosity. To our horror, the mate, sporting an evil looking grin on his face, dug a gaff (a giant, sharp hook with a handle) into its lower jaw and pulled it halfway aboard. The proud fisherman then pulled out a bowie knife and sliced the shark from anus to throat in one smooth motion. They then let the shark slide back into the water where we witnessed an actual feeding frenzy in the middle of a red, boiling putrid broth of shark stew.

All of us, including the captain and his mates, were appalled at the behavior and started screaming at the men. They simply ignored us and continued with their slaughter. There was nothing we could do. I couldn't help but wonder in the back of my mind if what we were doing was much better.

We continued to fish for the rest of the day and finally caught the smaller sharks we were hoping for. All of our boxes were filled with the dank water from the Bay. We headed in with our catch occasionally pressing down with our thumb on each of the shark's caudal peduncle (the area just in front of the back fin) that caused the sharks to gently swim forward enough to get the circulating air bubbles into its gills. It was four in the afternoon when we docked, and the sharks weren't doing well. As quickly as possible, we transported the sharks in stretchers to the back of a truck where we had "fresh" seawater from the dock pumped in. Most of the sharks had stopped breathing altogether, and we were very saddened. We tried desperately to revive them and took off for Connecticut with only an hour's sleep in the last 30 hours.

Joe and I were disheartened after so much effort and talked about how we might overcome the obstacle of the dirty water if we got to do this again. We decided that a better idea might be to bring along powdered artificial sea salts. The Mystic Marinelife Aquarium and its sister aquarium in Niagara Falls were originally built to prove that *Instant Ocean®*, a commercial brand of artificial seawater, actually worked. The Mystic Marinelife Aquarium was situated near the ocean, but it utilized *Instant Ocean* in all of its exhibits except for the marine mammals. These animals, it was thought, didn't need such a complex formula.

Additionally, I heard a lecture about the so-called sleeping sharks that Dr. Eugenie Clark had discovered. She described the phenomenon as a *narcoleptic* (sleep-inducing) effect due to the water conditions in underwater caves in Borneo. The lower *specific gravity*, or concentration of salt in the water, coupled with an increase in oxygen seemed to put the sharks to sleep slowing their breathing. It showed, for the first time, that not all sharks had to continually swim. With some adjustments to the box design, we were able to successfully capture and transport a small blue shark to the Aquarium. Blue sharks are members of the *Requiem* family, and, it was thought that these animals had to swim or die. If *these* sharks could be transported this way, then there would be no obstacle to bringing in the sand bar and sand tigers. By adding a small amount of sodium bicarbonate to the water we were able to prevent the mucous sloughing we had seen and a second trip was successful. We now had sharks swimming in our thirty-thousand-gallon Open Ocean exhibit!

I still remember the voice that would play over the Public Address system on a loop over and over again as you passed the front of the exhibit. It said something about the shark being the "swimming nose." This is in reference to their sensory organs located on their snout that can detect minute amounts of blood in the water over miles of open ocean and hone in on their prey. This is why chumming is so successful and also why you don't want to be in the water when you chum. Complementary organs also detect the movement in the form of electrical currents.

I remember when the movie *Jaws* came out. I often went into the Open Ocean exhibit with the sharks and cleaned the bottom of the tank by breaking up any accumulated detritus—mats of organic material that were the result of the mechanical filtration taking place in the sub-gravel filter. A movie crew from one of the local television stations filmed me performing this function and then interviewed me. They asked what I thought about swimming with sharks given the scare the movie was causing. I had to sheepishly admit that I hadn't seen the movie. The reason I gave was that I didn't want to scare myself out of a job.

They also asked what advice I would give to people if they found themselves in the water with sharks. I'm sure they were expecting something like, "splash around and that'd scare them off!" With the shark's ability to sense movement, that wouldn't be such a great idea. Just act like a wounded, helpless animal, and the shark will swim off. Sure. That's a little like dragging a McDonald's bag full of burgers and fries down the street in front of a bunch of fifteen-year-old boys. There's no quicker way to invite a shark to dine out—with you as the main course!

So, I looked directly into the camera and with all of the expertise and experience from someone who just a few weeks ago caught his very first shark and said, "I'd get out of the water as quickly as possible!" Hey, they had me on the spot! I *had* to sound like I knew what I was talking about. After all, I was just swimming with the things!

The peculiar thing about sharks in captivity: they don't usually exhibit the same kind of aggressive tendencies as in nature. I remember reading somewhere that it had to do with *pheromones*, a secretion of the skin of animals (and people) that had an effect on the sharks. We found out just how complete this was one day to my embarrassment. I had been to the New England Aquarium in Boston where they had an impressive Open Ocean exhibit that made ours look like a big goldfish bowl. The sharks were enormous! They swam right up to the divers and took fish from their ungloved hands. I was impressed! I also came back to Mystic with the idea that, if they can do it, why can't we?

I convinced Joe and our Vice President that it would be a great addition to the Aquarium, and we scheduled our first feeding demonstration. I suited up in a diving suit and a

Hookah mouthpiece that is sort of like a SCUBA mouthpiece but is fed by an air compressor from the surface. It gives you a continuous supply of air and is less cumbersome than a tank in such a small enclosure.

I filled a plastic bag with smelt, a species of freshwater fish, ahead of time and planned on hand-feeding the sharks. An announcement was made over the PA system well in advance and at intervals leading up to the feeding. The place was packed that day and, as I situated myself on the bottom, I could see the many expectant faces pressed up against the aquarium glass in eager anticipation of the exciting event unfolding before their very eyes. I came to learn that there were ulterior desires in the eyes of many of those watching. I hate to admit it, but I think some were hoping *I* was the food source. I know that's a terrible thing to say about people, but based on the visitors' behavior I observed over the years, you would probably agree with me.

The first thing I noticed right off, being the kind of observant person I am, is that there wasn't a shark in sight. In fact, there wasn't even a fish anywhere near me. The tank is only so big, so they couldn't have gone very far, I thought. Maybe they were just afraid since they weren't accustomed to being fed in this manner. Perhaps they didn't hear the announcement. We made them often enough. Maybe sharks don't hear as well as they smell. I decided *that* was the problem and that as soon as I brought out a succulent, fresh fish and waved it in the water, they'd swim right over and try and take my fingers off.

I pulled out a few fish and waved them around. The crowd was still with me, although I could clearly see they were beginning to lose interest. I was getting a little frustrated myself and began breaking up the fish and causing the water to become bloody all around me. Wait! Was this a good idea? What if I started a feeding frenzy? I vividly remembered the slaughter I had seen in Cape May and didn't really want to be in the middle of such an event. That, however, seemed to be the farthest thing from their minds.

People were starting to leave. I could see the disappointment in their faces. Some of the younger children stayed hoping things would improve. I decided to go and look for the sharks myself. I think I remember calling to them through my mouthpiece.

"Here, sharkie. Come and get it. Nice bloody, delicious fish. You're making me look stupid. Come on, boys. Okay. I am stupid. But just eat."

As you might imagine, they weren't buying it. The closer I got, the farther away they swam. The tank was circular, and I was just going in circles throwing fish into the water column over my head like I was showering a bride and groom with rice. After a few minutes, I realized the futility of my effort and that it was just me, the fish, and one very depressed looking little girl whose face was smudging the outside of the glass which, incidentally, I was now going to have to go out and clean. Would there be no end to my indignities? I learned the answer to that question many times over in the course of my working with the animals of the sea.

Now, back to our less than stellar arrival from Cape May.

We stopped about an hour outside of Cape May on our return trip to check on the sharks. Imagine how we felt when we opened the door to our U-Haul rental truck to find all of the sharks had died. We wanted to cry. They hadn't even survived the first leg of the journey. We drove the rest of the utterly depressed stopping frequently for coffee to stay awake. We arrived early the next morning, and, fortunately, there was no reception committee waiting for us. That would have been too much to deal with. It seemed we had fared no better than the beer guzzling shark killers we had scorned earlier. We would get better, but not before making many more mistakes.

Several years later, I performed a study that would eventually reveal the cause and subsequent cure for goiter in sharks in captivity. It turned into a 6-year-long study and involved other species of fish as well. The disease confounded researchers for decades. It was labeled hypothyroidism, and it only occurred in marine fishes (goiter). Other public aquariums, including the New

England Aquarium in Boston, dealt with the problem in sharks.

Most of the literature written by doctors and other researchers presumed it had to do with a lack of iodine, which was partly right. However, there was plenty of iodine in the water and food. My hypothesis was based on my knowledge and background as an aquarist rather than any knowledge of anatomy and physiology. I looked at the problem as an environmental one. The obvious (to me, anyway) factor was the presence of nitrate, the end product of nitrification taking place in all aquariums. In a freshwater aquarium, the nitrates are reduced by plants. Nitrates are plant food; check any bag of fertilizer. However, in marine aquariums, plants are prohibitively challenging to cultivate. Consequently, the nitrates must be removed by dilution.

I graphed all of the water chemistry for several years, and it stood out prominently compared to the rest of the chemistries. In six years of graphed data, all of the other parameters were either non-existent or negligible. As a result, we realized that the weekly water chemistry tests conducted by our lab tech were of no use. Unfortunately, we didn't need our tech anymore, and she lost her job. I was sorry to see her go because she was a pleasant coworker, and I learned a great deal about chemistry from her. However, the data on nitrates was peculiarly specific to each species of fish. I took over the responsibility of testing for nitrates using a spectrometer and, within a short time, was able to predict the appearance of goiter for each species.

One fish, the yellow-headed jawfish (*Opistognathus aurifrons*), displayed quite observable signs of the disease due to an unusual configuration of its thyroid. In most fish, the thyroid is more of a diffuse conglomeration of thyroid tissue, whereas, in the  jawfish, it is a bilobed organ reminiscent of a mammalian. It is also very sensitive to the accumulation of nitrates in the water system. To prevent them from displaying tumors, which often made it impossible for them to eat, we had to change the water frequently. In more than 20 species of fish, including sharks, we were thus able to prevent the goiter.

One of my test subjects was a lemon shark (*Negaprion brevirostris*). In one of my earlier experiments, I injected a synthetic thyroid hormone into the belly of a 4-foot lemon shark exhibiting lethargy and a prominent bulge under the  jaw characteristic of goiter. The next day when I checked on him, I was shocked to see him swimming rapidly around the circular Open Ocean exhibit like a hotrod off to the races! Apparently, it was an overdose. In three weeks, the shark slowed down, and the bulge diminished in size until it was gone completely. Since the synthetic sea salts we used were rich in iodine, clearly something was blocking the uptake of the critical element. In time, I discovered a wealth of information that proved my hypothesis was correct. Unfortunately, I never got to publish my findings except in an obscure paper at a small local college that only got me a single credit. It took another 10 years for a veterinarian from Canada to state what I had said earlier.

Chapter 8

WOODY

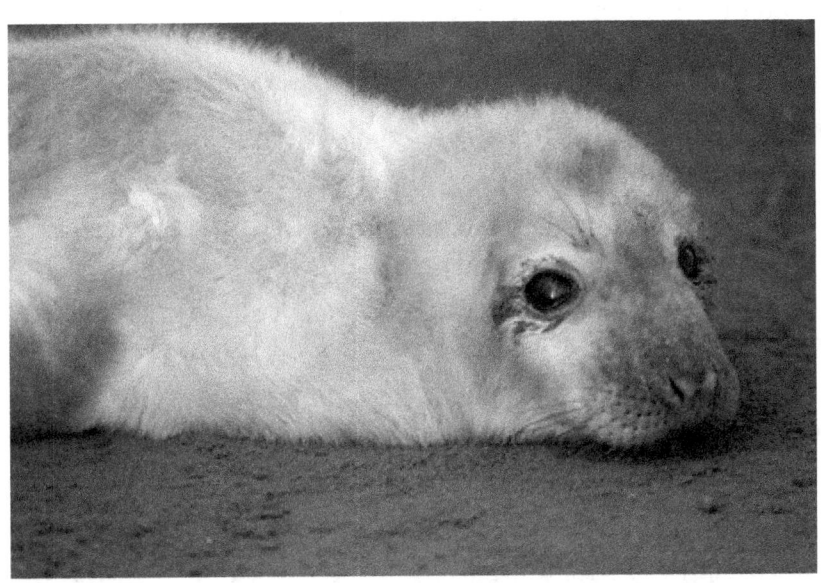

Surprises are the norm when working with wild animals. Sometimes aquarists will say, "...they bred wild this or that animal in captivity." It's a misleading statement. If people in captivity do their job right and provide all the necessary things the animal needs to feel like he's in his natural environment, they'll breed all on their own. We don't have to *breed* them. On the other hand, the term *husbandry* sometimes has a literal meaning!

It was the coldest day of the year. Nancy, one of our aquarists, and I were sitting inside a cardboard box on the visitor's side of the New England coast exhibit at Seal Island. It was 1:30 AM. We were bundled up as best we could but shivered with the bitter cold outside quickly seeping through the thin, fragile enclosure. Sips of hot coffee in a thermos made it bearable. We took turns looking through a flap we had cut out of a cardboard box situated on the visitors' side of the railing. We could just make out the form of a grey seal pup that had been born just minutes earlier.

Typically, new moms on the rookery learn about raising a pup from all of the other gray seal cows on the beach. Sydney had never given birth before, and we were concerned she wouldn't know what to do. There was no one to instruct her. Would she care for the pup? We simply didn't know, and we were taking every precaution.

Our job for the next few hours was to observe and watch for any nursing behavior. The temperature was in the single digits. Ice on the artificial beach made it difficult this time of the year to care for the animals. Reluctantly, we sprinkled the beach area with rock salt to keep from falling, but it ate away at the gunite (sprayed cement) surface of the exhibit and would erode it, requiring extensive repair work in the spring. But that was preferable to falling and becoming seriously injured.

The snow had fallen the day before and left a beautiful New England scene. Evergreens, with long branches, jutted out over the exhibit and created ominous shadows like giant scary monsters lifting their clawed arms. Snow dotted the rocks surrounding the exhibit as well. The rockwork served as a subtle fence to keep the animals from going over the exhibit wall into the murky water of the koi pond on the other side of the wall. There was enough light reflected from the night-lights not too far behind us to illuminate the beach for us to see shadows of the mom and pup. All was eerily quiet except for the sound of our breathing and the plumes of vapors from our breath in the cold air.

Around 2:00 AM, the pup began to move around. Every time it approached its mom, she would move away. It wasn't an encouraging sign, but we remained hopeful. The pup disappeared from our view behind an island also densely planted with towering evergreens. On the other side of the island, I knew there was a shallow pool area specifically designed for young pups to learn to swim, but in nature, this usually takes a couple of weeks.

I heard what I thought was a splash and became concerned. I grabbed a flashlight and chanced, shining it on the beach as cautiously as possible. I didn't want to spook the new mom. We waited for what seemed like an hour but, in reality, was only a minute. I almost decided to invade the beach when the pup appeared from around the corner and moved toward mom again. She moved away, but the pup persisted and appeared to nuzzle in. We couldn't be sure the pup was nursing, but I decided to wait until daybreak to grab the pup and bring it inside for a physical and weight check. At least that way we'd have a baseline to determine if the animal was nursing and gaining weight which should happen rapidly.

For the next few hours, nothing changed. Nancy and I took turns, heading into the building to warm up and get a fresh cup of coffee. As the sun began to peek over the horizon behind us and illuminated the beach, we could now see that the pup was some distance from mom and appeared to be shivering. It was time to find out what was happening.

I slid the large door to the exhibit quietly to the left. Another large door adjacent and to the right led to the California Coast exhibit. To the left of that was a small fenced-in holding tank. I could see the pup and decided to run onto the beach, grab it, and bring it inside for evaluation.

Mom and all of the other seals were obviously startled by my mad dash, and all of them scurried into the water with a splash. They were all barking what I would assume were insults at me. I ignored them and scooped up the pup in my arms and ran inside. I noticed right away the pup was a male. He looked up at me with *huge* big, black, saucer eyes that seemed to question who or what I was.

I set him down on the cement just inside the door as Nancy closed it behind us. There was a sickening "clunk" as his rear flippers made contact with the cement floor. I knew right then that the decision had been made for us. The little guy *had* fallen into the water, but I would *never* have expected his flippers to freeze solid!

We took the pup over to the main aquarium building, and I put a call into our staff veterinarian. He rushed right over. We both agreed that soaking the flippers in lukewarm water would be the first order of business. Rapidly heating them would have caused more damage.

While Nancy soaked the flippers, I busied myself locating a formula for feeding seal pups. I had one of our aquarists run over to the local convenience store and pick up all of the heavy cream he could get his hands on. I ground up some fresh frozen herring and added copious amounts of herring oil. This is definitely *not* the kind of diet you want to be on to lose weight. A seal's milk is exceptionally high in fat content. The young pup would need to build up a blubber coat quickly if he were to survive the winter months and frigid waters. I added a multi-vitamin complex and additional thiamine (B1). Animals on a frozen fish diet ingest an unusually high amount of thiaminase from the breakdown of the cells in the frozen fish. This can destroy thiamine and cause all kinds of problems with any captive animal that eats this kind of a diet, so we always supplemented our diets with this vitamin.

Once I had the "baby" formula ready, I needed to get it into the pup. An article I read indicated that sometimes a fur-type coat with a glove sticking through it might be accepted. It sounded good in theory. We all rummaged around and came up with a fur-lined parka. There were plenty of rubber gloves around, so I filled up a container and attached the glove with a hole in the fingers. I went up to the pup, and we tried numerous times. He wasn't buying it.

By this time, our vet had arrived and took a small blood sample to look for signs of infection. The blood indicated the pup was dehydrated, so the decision was made to intubate, that is—put a tube down into the pup's stomach and feed him directly. We used a large device with a plunger for icing cakes and attached a clear plastic hose. I held the pup in my arms and opened his mouth with a gloved hand. The teeth were small but very sharp. He was surprisingly strong. The vet inserted the tube to what he ascertained was the stomach and pushed the plunger slowly until all of the formulae was out.

We repeated this throughout the day a few times, but as late afternoon approached, we realized the feeding was going to have to continue through the night. I was already exhausted, but no one else felt comfortable with the responsibility of putting a tube in the pup's stomach and pumping in the baby seal formula we had concocted. So, I decided that my wife Pam, who was also an aquarist, and I would take the pup home and feed him in our bathtub. At least that way, I hoped, I would get some sleep.

We were renting a house in Stonington Village, a fancy shoreline community, at the time, and one of the rules was "No Pets." *Technically*, the pup wasn't a pet, so it seemed okay to me at the time. After all, we had two Capuchin monkeys in the house already. Pam was training them to work with handicapped people. They really weren't pets, either. Now I must admit our boa constrictor, and Conure parrot might have been stretching it a bit (you should have seen the look on the faces of some potential renters when we had decided to move out. I thought our landlady was going to kill us! She did keep our security deposit and rightly so).

We successfully snuck the pup into the house. There were no neighbors around when we got home, and it was dark. I fed the pup with Pam's help, and we set up a small corral at the foot of our bed with some luggage. It was a wooden floor, so we figured it would be easy to clean in the morning. I hoped he would sleep through the night.

Pam and I settled in, and the pup seemed secure enough. We gave him some towels to snuggle up with. Then we both fell asleep at about 11:00 PM. About 2:00 in the morning, I awoke to a strange sound. I still had the seeds of sleep in my eyes and a fog over my head and couldn't figure out what it was. It sounded like, "Maaaa! Maaaa!" I shook Pam from sleep and said, "What the heck is that? Someone's calling for their mother!"

Pam looked at me like I had gone insane. "Go back to sleep. You're dreaming."

Then *she* heard the cry, "Maaaa! Maaaa!" At the foot of the bed, there was a ruckus. The sound of luggage flying in every which direction startled us into action. When I turned the light on, the pup was heading out of the bedroom door and would be downstairs in no time. Pam and I started laughing. It was time to feed the baby. I looked at Pam and said, "He called for you. It's *your* turn!" Pam agreed and sat in the tub while I prepared the formula. Our home was starting to smell an awful lot like a rookery. I hoped we'd at least be able to get the smell out of the bedroom!

The next morning, we woke up and fed the pup yet again. At least we knew who was calling this time. Looking out the window of the small side street in Stonington Village, I saw a very picturesque sight. There was freshly fallen snow everywhere. We had gotten about six inches that night. Stonington Village is a quaint little town that has managed to retain the flavor of its early whaling village history. It is dotted with small shops and coffee houses and is very peaceful and quiet. It's also small enough for everyone to know your business. I wondered how we were going to get the pup out of the house without being seen. I came up with a brilliant plan!

We wrapped the pup up in a baby blanket after I had gone out and cleared the snow away from the company vehicle. I was glad I had taken it since our purple Gremlin we referred to, as "The Grape" might not have made it out in the snow. Stonington Village didn't plow very quickly, and the streets were treacherous after a snowstorm. With the Suburban running, I went back into the house and planned to rush to the car as quickly as I could. Unfortunately, one of our neighbors was shoveling his walkway and spotted us. Undoubtedly drawn to the "newborn baby," he headed in my direction. I tried to wave him off, saying I was in a hurry and didn't want the baby to catch a cold. He was determined and had that look people get around babies. The "Aw, isn't he cute!" look.

As he got within a couple of feet, the pup's "horse head-like" face became exposed as the wind blew the blanket back. Our neighbor stopped dead in his tracks, and his mouth dropped. I wrapped the blanket back over the pup's head and apologized, "Sorry, gotta go!"

I have no idea to this day what went through that poor man's mind. He probably thought we had a deformed baby, but he didn't dare to ask. In fact, he avoided us after that.

We took Woody (for the life of me, I can't remember where we came up with that name) back to the aquarium and continued to nurse him throughout the day. He was gaining weight rapidly, and we were encouraged. However, the skin on his rear flippers began to fall off. Our veterinarian determined that the flippers had become infected. The only way to save Woody was to amputate them.

Woody survived the procedure and continued to take formula. We never did chance taking him home again, and several of us took turns coming back to the aquarium at prescribed intervals to feed him. The surgical site healed well and, after a couple of months—we had Woody eating whole herring and mackerel—we introduced him into the New England Coast exhibit. Sidney, his mom, showed no interest in him, but that seemed okay—he was holding his own. We wondered if he would be able to swim and were delighted at how quick he adjusted. He seemed to be just as fast without his rear flippers since he was using his entire body and front flippers to propel him through the water.

The last report I got about Woody is that he went to another aquarium somewhere and had become the father of several pups!

Chapter 10

GURGLE, GRUMBLE, AND GRONK

Can you imagine having your nose hanging in your mouth all your life? That doesn't sound very pleasant, yet that is exactly what the adult male, elephant seal has to contend with. No wonder they get so grumpy! Well...not all of them. The distinctive personalities of animals were never more apparent than when someone at the Mystic Aquarium arbitrarily named three baby Northern Elephant Seals that had arrived for our California Coastline exhibit at Seal Island back when it first opened.

There has always been and probably will always be a

controversy about naming animals in public institutions like zoos and aquariums. One of our directors was dead set against this. So much so, in fact, that he named one of our sea lions, "No Name." After another of our aquarists named one of the seals something he felt was too *cutsie*, he named a sea lion after *her* and called it, *Betsy Rat*. However, that was nothing compared to naming three of our elephant seals, Gurgle, Grumble, and Gronk! Boy, did he have a canary!

I have to admit; I thought it was a little overboard — that is — until I got to know them better. They couldn't have been more aptly named had we known them for years.

Grumble was the female of the trio. She was a petite little thing around 400 pounds. With gigantic saucers for eyes, she would stare at you as if *you* were from another planet. Grumble liked to complain. No offense, ladies, but Grumble wanted her fish cut *precisely* the way *she* liked it — or she wouldn't eat at all for the rest of the day. You only got one shot at getting it right, and it had to be cut to her specifications as follows: 1) tail first, 2) cut diagonally but only from the bottom of the fish to the top, 3) top of the fish must be 5" while the bottom no more than 2" and finally, 4) you may only feed her if she likes you. Needless to say, Grumble was svelte for an elephant seal.

Long before the football player for the New England Patriots of the same name became famous, Gronk reminded me of Oscar, the Grouch on Sesame Street. He was always in a foul mood. I'll never forget the day when I had to treat an eye infection he developed with a little topical ointment. It was frigid outside, and I couldn't get the ointment out of the tube to dribble in his eye as I fed him. Usually, it wasn't a problem. I got the bright idea of squeezing the ointment into a syringe and heating it up with warm water. I planned on dribbling it onto his eye by gently pushing on the plunger. There was no needle on the syringe, of course.

It was *so* cold, however, that when I finally got Gronk close enough to feed him, the ointment was already too cold to squeeze out. I pushed on the plunger with all my might and then—pop—out came the whole thing in one big blob. It hit Gronk smack in the middle of the forehead, and you would have thought I just shot him. His eyes became wide with horror, and he went squealing across the pool and wouldn't come back the rest of the day.

Gurgle, on the other hand, was the gentlest marine mammal I ever had the pleasure of working around. He loved to eat, and he didn't care what type or size fish you gave him. Elephant seals have prehensile front flippers. That is to say, they can manipulate them like a hand. Gurgle was trained to raise himself up on his back hips and put his flippers around my shoulder while planting a somewhat wet kiss on my cheek. It should have scared all of the girls away, but Gurgle was actually responsible for my getting married. How so?

One of our aquarists was as enamored with Gurgle as I. She used to jump on his back and ride him from the top of the exhibit entrance all the way to the pool's edge. Gurgle looked forward to this and waited for the young woman named Pam to feed him every day at 10:00 AM. Pam even enjoyed the wet kisses Gurgle would plant on her cheek. To me, it looked like a match made in heaven!

But Pam was tall and beautiful with long brown hair and striking blue eyes. Would she go for a short little guy like me? Well, one day, Pam and I were chatting about Gurgle when I gave my best imitation of him responding to me calling his name. Okay, who would have thought that imitating an elephant seal would make a beautiful woman fall in love? However, the look in her eyes at that moment was priceless. Over forty years later, Pam's eyes still sparkle when I imitate Gurgle.

It is incredible to me how well marine mammals respond to individuals. I could stand in the middle of a crowd on the public side of the fence with the visitors all doing their best imitation of a sea lion's bark and simply say, "Gurgle!" His head would pop right up from a sound sleep, his eyes wide with anticipation and look all around for me. Each aquarist seemed to be able to develop his or her own rapport—a special relationship—with the animals. Well, except maybe Bob. Bob never could tell if the fur seals were done eating until one of them came up and bit him in the leg (which happened more than once). I heard that Bob was bitten by a shark in another public aquarium sometime after leaving Mystic. Maybe he would have been better off behind a desk or feeding goldfish. Not everyone is cut out for working at a public aquarium.

Several years after leaving Mystic, I returned to visit and went behind the scenes to see some of the animals I had worked with. I wondered if they would remember me, but I didn't have any high expectations. What a surprise when I went up to an adult harbor seal by the name of Susie. I asked if I could feed her, and they gave me a bucket of fish.

"Susie!" I said. She immediately ran over to me (okay, undulated over to me) and vocalized.

"Ahhh! Ahhh!" she said. It was her way of acknowledging me.

I gave a few typical commands that all trainers use, and she responded by waving and rolling over and bobbing her head up and down as I gave each queue.

Then I tried commands that only I knew. Susie responded by doing her imitation of Gurgle: raising her body was up on her hind flippers and trying to put her flipper around me while giving me a kiss.

The other aquarists all looked shocked. "We didn't know she knew how to do that! How did you get her to do it?"

Even *five* years later, I bumped into Susie who was now at the Norwalk Aquarium, where I was hired as a consultant. Susie remembered me still and even had a couple of pups I taught to do the Gurgle imitation!

"Is he dead?"

"No. Elephant seals can hold their breath for close to an hour."

"I think he's dead. You just don't want to tell us!"

Poor Gronk. He just loved to sleep on the bottom of the pool, utterly oblivious to everything around him. But the visitors always insisted we wake him or *they* wouldn't be able to sleep at night. So, I'd have to go and get a net and use the handle to prod poor old Oscar the Grouch out of his dream-filled sleep to satisfy the concerns of our visitors. Maybe that's why Gronk was always so grouchy?

Chapter 12

THE SOPRANO

Sometimes, we simply don't see problems coming until they are staring you right in the face—or in this instance—other parts of our anatomy. Here's a perfect example of what I mean.

One of our animal handlers was putting Squirty, one of our California sea lions, through his repertoire with him seated at the base of the stairway leading to the cliff in the California Coastline exhibit. To reach this area, Donna had to access from a door located under the cliff, step out onto a small rock island and then jump over to the cliff area. There was a shallow pool adjacent to this, and one had to be careful not to slip into it.

Also, in the exhibit, were about a dozen other sea lions and three juvenile elephant seals. A second handler worked with the adults on an opposite beach that was entered through another large sliding door. Donna was working Squirty and a few other young sea lions that had taken up their assigned "seats" on varying rocks surrounding the base of the cliff. It is easy to become distracted when working these many animals at the same time. If you ignore one for what it perceives as too long, it will leave its seat and run rampant through the other animals and disrupt the session. Donna lost her focus for a second when one of the pups bolted. She was in the process of giving Squirty a piece of fish as a reward.

Animal handlers are trained to exercise caution when handing a piece of fish to a seal or sea lion. It is necessary to keep fingers tucked away from the mouth to prevent being accidentally bitten by a mouth full of sharp, jagged teeth. Even a pup can exert a tremendous amount of force and cause severe damage. To make matters worse, their mouths are filled with a broth of microorganisms, any one of which can cause a nasty infection and lead to life-threatening situations.

Now, Squirty didn't have a nasty bone in his entire body. I have even stuck my head in his mouth. Okay, I'm not proud of that, but I wanted to make a point that he was exceptionally well trained. Squirty grabbed Donna's hand in the ensuing confusion to eat his reward before one of the young pups could run up and try to grab it. As he chomped down on Donna's hand, she reacted the way just about anyone would have, including me under similar circumstances. She yelled, "No!" With Squirty, this command had a very specific meaning, and he simply obeyed since he wanted to get another reward. So, he promptly followed orders by shaking his head with great enthusiasm. Problem was he still had Donna's hand in his mouth.

Donna kept yelling at Squirty, "no, no, no!" This was having a detrimental effect on Donna's hand. Fortunately, Squirty let go before any serious damage. Donna was very fortunate. I, however, had a similar encounter with Squirty and, if I had reacted as Donna had, there would have been more significant consequences than losing a hand.

It was only a couple of weeks later when I went out onto the beach to work with the sea lion group that included Squirty. I was in a bathing suit since I had been diving in the pool earlier to do some routine maintenance. Sea lions are voracious eaters, and they are easily trained because of their appetite. In some cases, they have even grabbed a handler as they turned to leave. Not out of aggression; more like, "I want more food buddy, and you're not leaving until I get!" It happened to my wife, Pam. She raised her hands up to indicate the signal that the food was gone and the session was over and said, "That's all!" Usually, there isn't any argument. As she turned to leave, however, a female California sea lion named Hope came up and sunk her teeth into Pam's jeans puncturing the skin in the process. The doctors and nurses at the emergency room got a big kick out of that. Pam wasn't able to sit comfortably for several days, and I teased her mercilessly.

When I had finished working with Squirty and the gang, I gave them the "That's all!" signal and everyone dove into the water—except Squirty. He dove into the shallow pool right behind me as I turned to leave. I heard the splash but didn't think much of it. Apparently, Squirty was ravenously hungry that day and just didn't want me to go. I stepped across to the small island of rocks with one foot behind and the other on the island when, out of nowhere, Squirty came straight up between my legs and locked onto to—shall we say—a rather sensitive area!

There was a large crowd of visitors watching this drama unfold with intense curiosity. If I had said, "No!" as Donna had done, well, I guess you can imagine the outcome: *Vienna Boys Choir*—soprano. Instead, my reaction, by a fluke of circumstance was less than controlled. Every man will immediately identify with my response. I said, "AHHHHHHHHHHHHH!!!" Coincidentally, that was the command for Squirty to open *his* mouth and say, "Ahhh." We had trained this behavior to examine Squirty's throat and teeth. When I realized Squirty had let go, I disappeared out the door in a blur. By the time Squirty looked for his reward, I was in the food prep room hyperventilating and considering what almost happened. I shuddered at the thought.

Chapter 13

BOTTLENOSED DOLPHINS

Most visitors to public aquariums eagerly anticipate seeing the dolphins with their perpetually smiling face. Little do they realize that even these beautiful and docile animals can have a dark side.

Working with marine mammals is the most exciting part of a job like this. Harry, our head trainer, got to go to Florida (while the rest of us were working our butts off getting the building ready for opening) and work with four newly acquired dolphins that were going to reside at Mystic. He worked with another professional trainer and was taught how to continue the process once he returned with the animals. I remember the excitement of going to the airport to pick up the dolphins. Four large crates dripping with water were unloaded into the back of a tractor-trailer. Inside, covered with a slimy substance we learned was zinc oxide to protect their delicate skin from being damaged, were the dolphins resting comfortably in a sling designed to accommodate them. The dolphin is an air-breathing mammal and is slightly more at ease out of the water than the shark, but not by much. A refreshing spray of water was misted over the animals to keep them from overheating.

I remember the feeling of awe that came over me when I sat next to them on the trip and had the responsibility of keeping them cool and watching their breathing. Edward, our staff veterinarian, monitored their heart and breathing rate and I think he too was a little bit intimidated by the prospects of caring for such magnificent creatures. They seemed calm and relaxed. Their trust in humans is truly an amazing thing.

Once they arrived at the Aquarium, a forklift was used to lift them onto large carts with wheels, and they were pushed up to the marine theater where the crystal-clear water awaited them. The water wouldn't stay clear for long. Even the best filter systems in the world can have a hard time keeping up with the excrement and urine if you are swimming in what essentially is your own toilet bowl no matter how large that is. A professor I had in a marine ecology class in college once told us that pollution is simply misplaced natural resources. That is so true in the case of keeping animals and fish in captivity. The natural processes that the ocean affords can't readily be duplicated in a closed system aquarium, so additional measures must be taken to clean the water. In the marine theater, impressive looking rapid-sand filters filled with varying size gravel and sand filter the feces out of the tank and then the filters are *backwashed*. This is essentially the equivalent of flushing the toilet.

Chemicals, such as chlorine and alum, are added to the tank to keep the bacteria from getting out of control and clear the water. Some aquariums use ozonators, which purify the water in a sort of pollution control plant (located away from the animals) and help clean the water. The alum is a form of aluminum sulfate salt that bonds with organic material such as small pieces of fish and feces left floating and too small to become trapped in the rapid-sand filters, making the particles larger so they can become trapped. While the chlorine and ozone keep the bacteria in check, the water then becomes cloudy-looking. In a large 400,000-gallon tank does this looks especially unhealthy and aesthetically unpleasant. It would be an endless battle keeping the water clean that would involve a great deal of research over the years and the collaboration with chemists and biologists at local colleges and universities.

The four dolphins were each picked up by an in-house pulley system designed to move them into the pool. As they were hoisted into the air with their pectoral flippers hanging out of a specially cut hole on each side and their tail fluke anxiously flapping behind them, I think they could sense the excitement themselves as they anticipated the water. But how would they react to being confined in a small holding tank first?

They were placed in a smaller satellite holding tank adjacent to the main part of the aquarium. A barricade made of netting that revolved separated each animal. I think the original idea was to release one animal at a time. But the animals had other plans. You don't want to become fooled by the perpetually smiling mouth of the dolphin. There is an impressive set of dentures in that mouth.

One of the males chewed a hole in the netting, and I *think* I volunteered to go in and fix it. I say that because clearly, I didn't know what I was thinking at the time. I put on a SCUBA tank and nervously slid in with this seven-foot long animal that weighed about seven hundred pounds. I kept telling myself, "Flipper. Remember Flipper." It wasn't working. It was the male, Kimo, whose side I was on, and he swam agitatedly around the enclosure. There wasn't a great deal of room, but everyone assured me that it was safe. I noticed, however, that *I was the one in the water.*

It reminded me of the time in high school chemistry when my teacher asked me to place a ladle with a small amount of chemicals over a Bunsen burner. Then he asked the entire class to go out of the room and look through the glass. I thought, *do you think I'm the stupidest person in the class?* I shut the Bunsen burner off and put the ladle down and accepted the "F" he gave me for the project. The guy never like me much. Of course, having blown up the lab once already that semester, I guess I couldn't really blame him.

Again, I wondered, do these people I work with not really like me? Are they sending me in the tank so they can have my job after I've been eaten by this monster? Of course, it's safe for them! It's not they who are in the water and in danger of being eaten alive!

So, into the water, I went. Immediately I swam over to the net with a quick kick of my flippers. Maybe I could impress Kimo with my swimming ability. Compared to a dolphin, the best human swimmer looks like a drowning worm at the end of a fishing pole.

I examined the net and began to tie the loose ends of the net together. Then I remembered where I was. I looked behind me to see where Kimo was, and I didn't see him anywhere. Now, I know he couldn't have gotten out—he had to be there somewhere. It was at that moment that I heard a rather loud, clacking noise directly in my left ear. Odd. As I turned to see what the sound was, I came face to face with Kimo's long snout and a *close* look at his teeth that were the source of the sound.

So, exactly what was he trying to tell me? Later I learned it was Kimo's way of saying, "get the heck out of my face you rubber duck!" Kimo went on to become an exceptional performer, but he also became somewhat aggressive as he matured and interacted sexually with the females. No offspring was ever forthcoming, which is typical in captive dolphins that perform. Animals kept explicitly for breeding purposes have been successfully bred, and there was at least one calf born at Mystic over the years.

The dolphin holding cell proved to be a complete disaster and was eventually done away with, but not before it caused a fatality. I arrived early one morning as I usually did and immediately noticed something wrong in the dolphin holding pool. It's funny how you get a sixth sense in a way about things that aren't right. Your eyes take in and process things that your conscious mind hasn't even become aware of yet. Such was the case this morning. It didn't take me long to realize what was wrong. One of the dolphins was trapped in the net of the barricade. It looked like it had panicked and rolled and was now severely tangled.

Without hesitation, I raced to the top of the stairs, ran into the marine mammal prep area, and grabbed a knife from the counter. Shedding my shoes in flight, I dove into the water straight for the trapped dolphin. There were loud pops and whistles and the sound of gates opening and closing in my ears. I realized that these sounds were caused by the other animals trying to communicate that something was wrong. The sounds had been reported on by many researchers in the past.

Frantically I began cutting around the long snout that gives the "bottle-nosed" dolphin its name, but I soon realized that the dolphin was dead already. I continued to cut the net anyway and released the poor animal. I still wasn't sure who it was. I swam to the surface, and by then several members of the Marine Theater staff had joined me when they saw the commotion. If the animal had been alive, time would have been of the essence. Dolphins can't stay under water very long without rising to the surface to breathe. There are no secondary organs as in some fish that breathe air. Fish have gills. Mammals do not. Then, again, if it were alive, I would probably have been thrashed to death myself by the struggling animal. It wasn't a decision I stopped and thought about *before* I went into the water.

The first person to greet me when I came out was one of the women who worked in the theater, named Anne. I told her the animal was dead. She burst into tears, crying, and we held each other. It was a terribly sad moment. It turned out it was one of the female dolphins. Her name was Misty.

When working every day with animals professionally, you try and remain objective and have a sort of detached relationship with the animals in your care. It's not like having a pet. In nature, animals die; it's a fact of life (although that sounds a bit like an oxymoron). It's one thing having a single pet that dies and most people that have had pets know what I'm talking about. You have a funeral and mourn the passing of your "friend." But in the circle of professional animal keepers, whether zoos or aquariums, it is considered a sacrilege of sorts to have emotional attachments to your animals — especially if you're a guy! The women in this profession can get away with crying, and it is usually counted as "maternal." With guys, you're called "*anthropomorphic*." The first time I was accused of that, I didn't know what it meant! But it didn't sound like anyone was paying me a compliment. It simply means you think animals are people, and *that* is simply not professional behavior!

Over the years, I learned to ignore what *they* said.

Chapter 14

SASSY

Not too many animals rate a bronze statue like a Greek god at the entrance to an aquarium. However, that is precisely what one encounters in a visit to the Mystic Aquarium. Such is the impact that Sassy, a bottle-nosed dolphin had on visitors and employees alike. She certainly made an *impression* on me, as I will explain in a moment.

Dolphins first gained popularity in the early 1970s when it came to light that tuna-fishing boats were accidentally killing them in their nets. The television show *Flipper* brought the lovable mammal of the sea into people's homes, and public aquariums attracted millions of visitors and introduced the amazingly intelligent creatures up close. Their perpetual smile and phenomenal agility and speed won the hearts of people across the country and catalyzed a movement that eventually made the tuna industry stand up and take notice. People stopped buying tuna—until the government intervened and put agents on boats to monitor the fishing industry's activities. The result was the industry's implementation of techniques designed to save the dolphins and, hence, the advent of "Dolphin Safe" labels on tuna cans.

Among dolphins in captivity, Sassy was a standout—the Michael Jordan of the dolphin world. Talk about "air time!" Sassy was famous for racing across the bottom of the aquarium's huge 400,000-gallon marine theater pool, torpedoing up from the 18-foot deep water and leaping another 30 or so feet into the air. She was so good that trainers were concerned that Sassy might someday leap right through the roof—a real possibility. Veterinarians at the aquarium were also worried about the constant impact the landing, after a jump that high, might have on her and curtailed her jumping as she matured.

My encounter with Sassy happened one day during a routine physical. Typically, dolphins can be trained to offer their tail fluke for drawing blood for testing. It doesn't hurt them, and many of the dolphins were trained to cooperate. Sassy, however, had other ideas. She proved she wasn't named Sassy for nothing. No amount of coaxing or cajoling would convince her to offer up her tail fluke. We had no choice but to place her in one of the small satellite holding pools and drained the water. We tried approaching her under those circumstances, and she still wouldn't sit. Three hundred pounds of powerful animal is more than a match for us puny humans.

The USDA required the examination, so there was no getting around it. We had to come up with a way to take the blood sample. The plan was to have ten attendants: trainers, aquarists and maintenance people, jump Sassy all at the same time and immobilize her long enough to get her strapped into a stretcher. The gurney (I use the term loosely) was an army cot with solid oak handles. Along with seven, seatbelt-type straps, we assumed Sassy would be completely immobilized. We were wrong.

First of all, I got the tail fluke. Since I was only around 175 pounds (oh to see that day again!), Sassy flipped me around like I was a mosquito. I managed to hold on while a fellow employee who was considerably larger than I was jumped on. His 300 pounds added to my weight, and Sassy stopped fighting.

Once we had her securely strapped onto the stretcher, everyone stepped back except the head trainer and me. It was my job to keep a close eye on her breathing, so I was standing comfortably near Sassy's head. The head trainer was next to the tail fluke talking with the veterinarian who was busy preparing the tubes for collecting blood.

Now, the tail fluke of the dolphin is probably the most powerful part of the animal. Anyone who has ever seen one of these magnificent creatures quite literally walk on top of water holding their entire weight straight up in the air with no more than the tip of their tail fluke can appreciate just how powerful they are. We were all relaxed and figured that the ordeal was almost over—at least for another 6 months. Without any warning, Sassy contracted her entire body in one swift motion and snapped most of the seat belts, breaking the army stretcher in the process.

Sassy's powerful tail fluke caught our head trainer in the back and sent him literally flying into the side of the tank whereby he slunk to the floor unconscious. Sassy's head came up and caught me in the chest with a cracking sound leaving me gasping for air. I wound up with a bruised collarbone, and our head trainer had a concussion. The veterinarian had empty tubes, and Sassy swam off to the main pool to excite the crowds for years to come. I never went near her head again.

Chapter 15

JONAH

Religious or not, most people are familiar with the story of Jonah and the big fish. As the story goes, Jonah, a prophet of the nation of Israel, was sent by God to the nation of Nineveh to inform them of their imminent destruction. The Ninevites, however, were an unusually cruel people and Jonah was terrified they were going to torture and kill him. So, instead of heading to Nineveh, Jonah grabbed a ship in the opposite direction.

Determined to help Jonah fulfill his assignment, God sent a violent storm that threatened to destroy the ship and everyone on board. Apparently feeling guilty of putting the innocent sailors in danger, Jonah told them to throw him into the sea, and the storm would abate. They did, and the storm immediately ceased. Jonah, on the other hand, was swallowed by a large fish where he remained for three days and three nights.

On the third day, the fish vomited Jonah up back where he had started his trip whereupon, he immediately traveled to Nineveh to deliver God's judgment message. It turned out well for Jonah and, if you're interested in learning what happened, it's in the Bible under the book by the same name.

I tell this story because I had a similar experience. Okay, I exaggerate — a little. One of the marine mammals the aquarium acquired early on was a Beluga whale by the name of Alex. Alex was about seventeen feet long and quite old at the time — and completely blind. I don't remember the reason for the blindness, but it is a common problem among marine mammals in captivity. His name was Alex, and he was a lovable animal with a mild spirit about him. He was also quite intelligent, as are most cetaceans (whales, dolphins, and porpoises), comparatively speaking, perhaps on a scale with chimpanzees or even some dogs.

Alex, since he was unable to see, responded well to touch commands. For example, touching his blowhole on top of his head, where cetaceans' nostrils are located, elicited a spout of water. A tap on the mouth and Alex spewed out an enormous amount of water onto the stage of the Marine Theater. He had a bag of tricks, or behaviors, to demonstrate the unique adaptions to his handicap. We often swam with the dolphins and whales, rarely encountering any serious problems. However, occasionally, we had to drain the main pool of its 400,000 gallons to perform a variety of maintenance projects. Alex was trained to swim into a satellite pool so that the work could be accomplished. Or so we thought. Apparently, having experienced one previous trip into the much smaller pool was enough.

The day came when the scheduled maintenance was to take place. The trainers had tried every trick they could think of to entice Alex into the smaller pool; nothing worked. We were getting desperate. Then, Fred, the lead trainer had an idea. What if we lured him next to the entrance of the smaller pool and then jumped in from opposite sides of the gate and held his fluke to keep him from backing out? It was worth a shot. So, Fred and I donned snorkeling gear and positioned ourselves at the gate while another trainer coaxed Alex to the entrance. She tried several times in a last-ditch effort to get him to go involuntarily, but to no avail.

The next time Alex was lured to the pool entrance, Fred, and I were poised to jump. Emma, one of the trainers, kneeled down and waved a fish in front of the entrance. Alex inhaled it and backed away. Fred and I bided our time. Alex had to get at least half of his voluminous body through the gate for this to work.

Again, Emma enticed Alex, ever wary, to the entrance. Still, we waited. Fred told Emma, "One more time."

This was it. If we didn't get Alex into the satellite pool, we didn't have a backup plan.

Alex cautiously inched forward as Emma moved the fish past the opening just out of his reach. A little more, I thought. Come on, come on.

Fred yelled, "Now!"

We jumped and grabbed for the fluke. Instead, we both wound up tumbling in the water with an armful of nothing.

We surfaced, expecting to find Alex swimming off to the other end of the pool. Instead, we heard a "Woohoo!" behind us as Emma pushed the gate closed. Apparently, we had frightened Alex into the satellite tank.

Okay, so it didn't quite go as planned, but we succeeded in our objective. This time. Pool drains were a common occurrence. We wondered what would happen the next time we needed to drain the pool. My Jonah experience was yet to take place.

One of the satellite tank's gates became inoperable one day, and I volunteered to take a look. I never missed a chance to get in the pool with the marine mammals! I donned a mask and snorkel but passed on the flippers since I wasn't going to need them. Access to the gate was on the main poolside, and I slipped into the water and slid down one of the restraining poles where the gate was logged. The dolphins were in the opposite satellite tank, and only Alex was in the pool. Usually, he ignored people.

I was at the surface of the water using my snorkel and halfway between the satellite tank and the main pool examining the track where the gate was apparently stuck when, suddenly, I felt enormous pressure on my leg as if I was getting sucked into a giant vortex. I screamed, as much as one can scream with a snorkel in his mouth and jerked away from whatever it was that had me. It was Alex, and he had sucked my entire leg into his mouth!

I guess he was as surprised as I because he spit me out and bolted across the pool in a flash. Fortunately, for me, beluga whale teeth are conical and not particularly sharp. I sustained no injury except, perhaps, to my pride for screaming like a little girl.

I realized what had happened. Since Alex is blind, his sense of echolocation is particularly well-tuned to his environment; it is how he "sees." I can only imagine the confusion he must have felt when his sonar detected two dismembered legs sticking out from the wall of the main pool. Since whales have no hands, the only way they can feel is by using their mouth. It turned out that Alex was as surprised as I was when I jumped.

Poor Alex took it pretty hard, too. He sulked in the corner of the pool for three days before he came out and started eating again. I felt terrible for having frightened him, but I think anyone would have reacted the same way if they suddenly found a 17' beluga whale had swallowed their leg.

It wasn't the last time we had adverse interactions with Alex. Now that he was wise to our tricks for getting him into the satellite tank, he got stubborn. All our attempts failed. We tried stretching a line with weighted rope every couple of feet extending down to the bottom to simulate a net. Our thought was that he would assume it *was* a net and avoid it by escaping into the satellite tank. It didn't work.

Then we decided we get him close and jump him as we had done before, hopefully frightening him into the tank. That didn't work. However, he was hungry because we withheld food. It was imperative we get him out of the main tank since we needed to drain the entire pool to perform major repairs to the filtration system. I'm not entirely sure how it happened, but I wound up on Alex's back, basically riding him. It's not something we had ever done before. We never treated our marine mammals with what we thought were undignifying riding behaviors such as those performed at other Aquariums with killer whales (Orcas). However, there I was.

On instinct, I suppose, because it wasn't as if I had given any thought to it, I reached up and grabbed the bar that ran across the top of the gate and, as ridiculous as this sounds, I *pulled* Alex into the satellite tank far enough for him to swim the rest of the way in. There was no way that was ever going to work again! But the fun wasn't over.

With the main pool draining, we had the opportunity to remove Alex for a physical and bloodwork. I was holding the tail, but the others hadn't gotten into position yet when the next thing I knew, I was up in the air holding onto the tail fluke for dear life. However, Alex let me down gently, and the blood was drawn without any further incident. Soon, the work was completed on the filters, the pool filled, and everyone was happy.

Science and, consequently, knowledge has come a long way since those early days. A great deal has been learned about the behavior and physiology of beluga whales in captivity. While I'd rather see them in their natural environment, I suppose that's a selfish view having had the opportunity to work with these magnificent creatures up close and personal. It is something I will never take for granted.

Afterword

We live at a time like no other since man has been on the earth. The number of animals that have gone and will go extinct directly related to mankind's activity is astonishing. This is not a political statement as I am politically neutral. This is a statement based on years of observation and carefully examining the science behind the changes in the environment.

For example, the U.N. News article entitled, **"World is 'on notice' as major UN report shows one million species face extinction,"** states the following,

On at-risk fauna and flora, the study asserts that human activities "threaten more species now than ever before" – a finding based on the fact that around 25 percent of species in plant and animal groups are vulnerable.

This suggests that around one million species "already face extinction, many within decades unless action is taken to reduce the intensity of drivers of biodiversity loss."

Without such measures, there will be a "further acceleration" in the global rate of species extinction, which is already "at least tens to hundreds of times higher than it has averaged over the past 10 million years", the report states.

It notes that despite many local efforts, including by indigenous peoples and local communities, by 2016, 559 of the 6,190 domesticated breeds of mammals used.

This is an eye-opening comment from a multi-nation agency. Additionally, oil spills such as the Exxon Valdez in 1989 reportedly killed upwards of a half-million seabirds, as well as seals, whales, bald eagles, and sea otters. NOAA reports that there is still some 27,000 gallons of oil remaining in the sandy shores. In 2010, another massive oil spill in the Gulf of Mexico by the BP Deepwater Horizon dumped four and a half *million barrels* of oil causing untold damage. I watched in horror as an estimated 100,000 barrels poured into the beautiful, pristine waters. It sickened my stomach as I knew that the damage would be felt for decades to come in ways that we are just now realizing.

Add to the oil spills of only the couple I mentioned is the Fukushima Nuclear disaster in Japan. While not the result of a manmade accident, no one can stop the radiation still pouring into the Pacific Ocean, which will affect marine life for centuries! Even now, whales and dolphins are dying at unprecedented numbers, due to disappearing food sources (such as the anchovy). Peru recently suspended anchovy fishing season early due to dwindling catches.

Add to that the disappearing reef habitats and bleaching of corals at unprecedented rates, likely due to global warming. One cannot but wonder what the future will hold for the planet if these events continue to plague our home.

Despite my pointing out a few of the challenges facing the oceans on our planet, this story is about the awe-inspiring marine life I have had the absolute pleasure to have been associated with over my careers. Yes, that's plural. The two predominant careers have been as an Aquarist and then Curator at the Mystic Aquarium in Connecticut and as the Zebrafish Expert at Pfizer's Global Research and Development's Comparative Medicine Department in Groton, Connecticut from which I retired in 2016. These stories are a few of my more memorable ones from the Mystic Aquarium. I hope you enjoyed them!

John Benjamin Sciarra

APPENDIX

Mako shark (*Isurus oxyrinchus*) Illustration by
Keith M. Cowley

*The mako is one of the fastest sharks and
known to leap into the boats of unwary
fishermen!*

Natural History

Natural History—Sharks

Reality Check

People's perception of sharks has changed dramatically over the years, particularly since the movie, "Jaws," based on the bestselling novel by Peter Benchley. In 2014, on the 40th anniversary of Jaws an article written by Nancy Knowlton, and Wendy Benchley *stated, "In the public's mind, the fear of sharks that Jaws initially inspired was soon replaced by fascination, which continues to this day. Sadly, that fascination has been joined with despair over the last several decades, as evidence has accumulated that shark populations are plummeting, driven by overfishing. Peter Benchley often stated in later years that he could never again write a book like Jaws, and he devoted much of his post-Jaws career to ocean conservation."*

Numerous imitations of the man-eating monster with the anthropomorphic predilection for revenge followed with distorted sequels and, even worse, b-movie series for television such as "Sharknado," and many other grotesque manifestations of the animals. Sharks seemed to dominate the nightmares of adults and children alike, and a generation was born numbed from the exposure to these warped ideas of the true nature of sharks. Sharks, in fact, are beautiful creatures designed for a purpose and play a critical role in the world's oceans and are deserving of our respect and understanding.

The truth is, far more sharks are killed by humans than the converse. The International Shark Attack File (ISAF) posted by the Florida Museum (https://www.floridamuseum.ufl.edu/shark-attacks/yearly-worldwide-summary/) lists, "*130 incidents of alleged shark-human interaction occurring worldwide in 2018. Sixty-six cases represent confirmed unprovoked shark attacks on humans. Thirty-four of the remaining cases were confirmed as provoked attacks on humans.*" The site defines unprovoked attacks as "*...incidents where an attack on a live human occurs in the shark's natural habitat with no human provocation of the shark,*" and provoked attacks as "*...when a human initiates interaction with a shark in some way. These include instances when divers are bitten after harassing or trying to touch sharks, attacks on spearfishers, attacks on people attempting to feed sharks, bites occurring while unhooking or removing a shark from a fishing net, etc.*" In contrast, Forbes Magazine stated that over "***one million** sharks and rays were exterminated in 2017.*" It is apparent who the more dangerous species are.

Frequently, shark attacks are precipitated unknowingly by the actions of the attacked. Surfers and boogie-borders likely present as sea lions or seals to the apex predators of the oceans merely looking for a meal (53% according to the ISAF). While humans may not be the intended target, occasionally, severe damage and/or death may ensue before the shark realizes the unwary swimming dinner isn't to its liking.

Swimming in areas where seals, (such as Grey Seals and Harbor Seals in Cape Cod, Massachusetts) have resulted in attacks and deaths from shark bites. Great Whites, the object of the fear in the movie, "Jaws" (*Carcharodon carcharias*) frequent those waters due to the abundance of seals. Signs are posted up and down both sides of the Cape warning swimmers to be wary of swimming with seals nearby and of staying out of the water in the early morning and evening when sharks are most likely to feed. In 2018, a man was killed by a Great White there, still a rare occurrence by comparison with other human activities such as driving a car or interacting with man's "best friend;" the canine. Wikipedia lists **4.5 million** dog bites yearly with **6000-13,000 deaths** each year (2005 figures), while in 2018, according to Safer America, *"Every year, roughly 1.3 million people die in car accidents worldwide – an average of 3,287 deaths per day."*

Many of the sharks killed by fishermen are solely for the fins. The still-living shark is usually cast back into the ocean where it drowns, bleeds to death or is eaten by other sharks. Shark fin soup is a Chinese delicacy primarily served at weddings, expensive restaurants (often costing upwards of $200/bowl), and other special events (https://www.sharksider.com/shark-fin-soup/).

Fortunately, there are many organizations devoted to the protection and conservation of sharks working tirelessly to educate the public and change the culture and perceptions of sharks for the beautiful and magnificent creatures they are. Here are a few of the organizations where additional educational materials are available as well as ways to get involved. Also, below is a limited natural history of a few of the sharks mentioned as well as others in the stories from this publication.

Some Resources for Shark Conservation and Education

https://www.sharktrust.org/blog/creature-feature-white-shark

https://www.ocearch.org/about/

https://www.livingsharks.org/

https://www.floridamuseum.ufl.edu/search/?q=sharks

https://www.sharks4kids.com/

https://www.fisheries.noaa.gov/national/international-affairs/shark-conservation

Introduction to Sharks

It is estimated that sharks have been on earth for ~450 million years, long before the dinosaurs first appeared on land, belonging to the superorder *Selachimorpha*. Other *Chondrichthyes* of the subclass, *Elasmobranchii* include the skates and rays. Unique to the family of sharks of modern times is a cartilaginous skeleton with no calcareous backbone typical of all other fish.

Classification

Kingdom: *Animalia*

Phylum: *Chordata*

Class: Chondrichthyes

Subclass: Elasmobranchii

Superorder: Selachimorpha

Shark External Anatomy

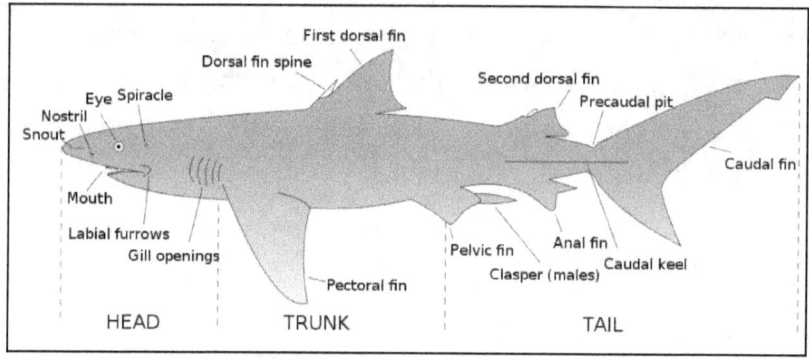

Wikipedia: Chris Huh

The shark species as we know them have been around for 100 million years; this means that they were dwelling the oceans when dinosaurs were roaming the land. In fact, dinosaurs came and left, but the humble, efficient shark continues to roam the oceans with only man as its chief predator.

Sharks are truly remarkable creatures, and not all hunt, eat, sleep, or reproduce the same way. There is as much variety among sharks as there are bony fishes with some 500 species of known sharks today. There are a plethora of websites devoted to the education of sharks. A few notable ones are mentioned above.

Most of the shark species are harmless and avoid human interaction. Of course, the most notable of the so-called man-eaters is the Great White (*Carcharodon carcharias*) due to its impressive size and sharp teeth (and association with the movie, Jaws). Most of the more publicized shark attacks have involved this magnificent creature, but knowledge is improving thanks to tagging/tracking efforts of organizations such as OSEARCH. Attacks are rarely purposeful on humans as mentioned earlier, but people are mistaken for prey.

Other sharks, such as the White Tip Reef (*Triaenodon obesus*), Blacktip (*Carcharhinus limbatus*), and Tiger (*Galeocerdo cuvier) are* known to attack divers invading these animals' territory. Usually, the sharks give a warning behavior; agitated behavior to ward off potential trespassers. Learning about sharks through education will engender respect and help dispel much of the misinformation about these animals leading to more significant conservation efforts. An ocean without sharks is in danger of dying, and the planet can barely handle man's mismanagement of its resources as it is.

Select Natural History

Lemon Shark – *Negaprion brevirostris*

Photo: Wikipedia by Albert Kok

DESCRIPTION

An average length of 8-10 feet, the lemon shark, uses its yellowish/brown color on its back as camouflage in shallow sandy bottoms. It can weigh as much as 550 pounds in adulthood. It is primarily an opportunistic, nocturnal feeder preferring fish, mollusks, and crustaceans, although an occasional bird or small shark may provide additional meals.

Lemon sharks are among the species sought for shark fin soup and are listed by the *IUCN (The International Union for Conservation of Nature and Natural Resources)* Red List of Threatened Species as of 2015, particularly in the waters off the coast of Florida, one of its primary habitats.

According to the Florida Museum website, *"Lemon sharks represent little threat to humans. According to the International Shark Attack File, there have been only 10 unprovoked attacks by lemon sharks, all occurring in Florida and the Caribbean. There have been no fatal attacks attributed to this species. The lemon shark inhabits coastal waters in close proximity to swimmers, surfers, and divers. While the number of attacks attributed to this species is low caution is still warranted as they are a large predatory species (ISAF 2018)."*

BEHAVIOR

While the lemon shark may wander off from a group, it is usually found in similar-sized groups of ~20. The lemon has been described as having a hierarchal structure which may facilitate breeding and hunting. Studies of the lemons' brain seem to indicate an ability to learn from one another and social dominance. They tend to rest sporadically on the bottom during the day, expending energy to pump water through their gills. They are more active at dawn and dusk.

The lemon attacks its prey by biting and shaking its head back and forth forcefully tearing off pieces of flesh. They prey primarily on fish, mollusks, and crustaceans as well as the occasional seabird.

REPRODUCTION

The lemon is viviparous (live-bearing) with the embryos developing inside the mother and feed on a yolk sac. In the spring and summer months, adults return to the same locations they were born to breed. Once the young are born, they use these areas as a nursery while they grow. The average gestation is a year or less with females mating with multiple males. Fertilization is internal.

CONSERVATION

Because of its gentle nature, *Negaprion breviostris* has been studied extensively with much of the research attributed to Samuel Gruber of the University of Miami. This author (Sciarra) has found that they do well in captivity except for the sensitivity to nitrate accumulation in closed-system aquariums. An iodide supplement may be all that is needed to prevent the occurrence of goiter where nitrates tend to build up between water changes. They tolerate the presence of humans both in the wild and in captivity well. As mentioned, caution should still be exercised around the larger specimens.

Its conservation status is "Near Threatened" on the Red List of the International Union for the Conservation of Nature (IUCN). No plans or programs are currently underway for its conservation. However, the United Nations International Plan of Action for the Conservation and Management of Sharks has some oversight and awareness of the status of the lemon shark.

Blue Shark – *Prionace glauca*

The Blue shark (*Prionace glauca*) is a beautiful, sleek-looking shark, with a blueish skin, and it is one of the most widely distributed sharks in the world. It is a member of the order *Carcharhiniformes*, of the family *Carcharhinidae* and the Genus *Prionace*.

DESCRIPTION

The blue shark is perhaps one of the most elegant and aerodynamic of the shark species. With its elongated, conical snout, and slender body, it is easy to recognize. Known as one of the *Requiem* sharks, it must swim continually to pass oxygenated water over its gills. Its two-toned coloration (bluish on top and white underbelly), gives this shark many distinctive features you wouldn't confuse with any other species. The blue sharks' pectoral fins are distinctly different from other sharks.

The adult may reach up to 13' in length and weigh in at over 500 pounds. The females are significantly smaller than the males.

BEHAVIOR

The blue shark is found in virtually every marine habitat around the world's oceans except Antarctica. Occasionally, sport fishermen have been observed catching blue sharks within eyesight of swimmers in Misquamicut, Rhode Island (author's experience). It is reported that they tend to inhabit deeper waters in the tropics.

The typically slow swimming predator can accelerate quickly when feeding on prey, which includes fish, squid, and, occasionally, the unwary seabird. The sharp triangular teeth are razor sharp and are used for tearing flesh from its prey.

REPRODUCTION

The Blue shark is viviparous and reaches sexual maturity at ~6 years old. The male inserts its clasper during mating into the female fertilizing the eggs. Gestation is between 9 months/year, averaging 50 pups that are on their own after birth.

CONSERVATION

Listed as "Near Threatened," according to the Red List of the IUCN, the blue shark is not a target for commercial fishermen. However, they may be unintended victims of commercial nets and can be the target of sport fishermen. It is also under the International Plan of Action for the conservation and management of sharks, the Sustainable Fisheries Act and the Code of Conduct for Responsible Fisheries from the Food and Agriculture

Organization of the United Nations Fisheries and Aquaculture.

The blue shark may also be the victim of shark-finning as there are no current plans to stem this practice on a global scale.

Sand Tiger — *Carcharias taurus*

The Sand tiger is the definitive example in ferocious *looking* sharks, but, despite the impressive set of choppers, it is quite docile. Attacks have occurred on humans only when provoked.

DESCRIPTION

The Sand tiger shark is a robust looking animal with gray to brown scaling on top and a whitish underbelly. They range in size from ~6 to 11 feet at adulthood and are often seen in public aquariums due to their docile nature, intimidating set of dentures, and ease of care. They can be found in temperate to tropical waters in most oceans, typically close to shore.

BEHAVIOR

These sharks have the unusual ability to swallow air at the surface as ballast, allowing them to remain stationary while hunting for prey. They have a voracious appetite and feed primarily on small fish, but are opportunistic predators, feeding at night. They hug the bottom and have been known to hunt in groups. It has been reported they will attack fishing nets full of fish, which wreak havoc for commercial fishermen.

REPRODUCTION

While technically viviparous, an unusual activity occurs in the ovum of the female after fertilization by the male (or males). Maturing fetuses are known to engage in embryonic cannibalism whereby the other embryos will eat their smaller littermates (Chapman et al.; Royal Society Publishing). Possibly due to this activity, this shark has a particularly low rate of reproduction with dangerously low population levels.

CONSERVATION

The IUCN Red Lists the Sand Tiger as "Vulnerable," and several organizations are actively engaged in conservation efforts including the Norwalk Maritime Aquarium in Connecticut where this author had assisted in the introduction of Sand tigers when it first opened (https://www.maritimeaquarium.org/conservation-projects). See the Aquarium's shark exhibit below.

It is possible that this shark could soon enter the endangered species list due to its low numbers in nature.

Natural History—Seals and Sea Lions

The California Sea Lion is probably the most well-known of all of the pinnipeds in the world because of their prevalence in zoos and aquariums. Often, these quite intelligent marine mammals are depicted as little more than trained clowns performing tricks for the delight and amusement of the paying public. While many institutions have recently made significant changes and used their resources for the conservation and education of these animals, the impression may still linger.

Hopefully, younger visitors to the modern Aquariums will have a better understanding of the natural behaviors and dignity that, as stewards of the world's oceans, much can be done now — immediately — to curtail the damage done to the marine animals' environment. Something as simple as stopping or reducing the use of plastics, eliminating the use of balloons in our many causes for celebration, and snipping the small plastic can holders used for six-pack sodas (and beer!) can save the lives of marine mammals from seals and sea lions to whales and dolphins!

A short introduction to the status of some of the animals discussed in the story will, hopefully, help to raise awareness of the uniqueness of these magnificent creatures.

Seals and Sea lions are categorized into two distinct families (Walrus are the exception belonging to their own family, *Odobenidae*), *Otariidae* (the eared seals: sea lions and

116

fur seals), and *Phocidae* (the earless seals, or true seals). First, let's take a look at the sea lion.

California Sea Lions

DESCRIPTION

The California sea lion (*Zalophus californianus*), one of six species of sea lions is primarily indigenous to the West Coast of North America. The males are distinct from the females with larger size, thicker necks and enlarged crest on their foreheads and can weigh up to 700 pounds with females around 250 pounds. They are distinct from the seals (*Phocids*) in that they have external ears, swim primarily with large front flippers and have a hinged hip joint allowing them to run on land. The *Phocids*, lacking this joint, undulate like a worm on land, although quite easily. In nature, it is estimated they live ~30 years. They feed on fish and squid and are prey to great white sharks and Orcas (Killer Whales).

BEHAVIOR

Sea lions are highly intelligent, and have been used by the military for a variety of tasks humans couldn't perform. For example, the U.S. Navy Marine Mammal Program studies the military use of marine mammals, including California sea lions, *"…and trains animals to perform tasks such as ship and harbor protection, mine detection and clearance, and equipment recovery. The program is based in San Diego, California, where animals are housed and trained on an ongoing basis. NMMP animal teams have been deployed for use in combat zones, such as during the Vietnam War and the Iraq War,"* according to Wikipedia®.

Marine mammals, in general, are highly adaptable and easily trained due to their ability to learn complex behaviors quickly. Most are food-motivated, giving the impression of affection which could be misleading if presented to impressionable minds, particularly young children. The California sea lion can be dangerous if not handled properly. Humans have been bitten when near adults hauled out on wharves in California where large numbers prefer to congregate. Interaction with wild sea lions should be discouraged.

REPRODUCTION

California sea lions haul out on sandy and rocky shores in breeding colonies, called harems although they frequent harbors, beaches, and docks. There is no familial structure once the pups are weaned. A remarkable ability is that the females and pups can recognize one another through distinctive calls, even among significant numbers in the rookeries. Sea lions, in general exhibit an unusual phenomenon called delayed implantation. After fertilization takes place, the blastocyst (the fertilized embryo with some differentiated cells) floats around in the uterus for several months before attaching to the uterine wall and develops. This allows the females to feed before returning to the rookery to give birth the same time each year, although gestation is actually around 7-8 months. They reach sexual maturity around 4-5 years.

CONSERVATION

The International Union for Conservation of Nature (IUCN) lists the species as "Least Concern" due to its robust population. However, with increasing infringement on its natural habitat by plastics, overfishing and pollution, entanglement in fishing nets, biotoxicity and other human activities, this could change.

Resources:

https://www.fisheries.noaa.gov/species/california-sea-lion

https://www.fisheries.noaa.gov/topic/laws-policies#marine-mammal-protection-act

Harbor seals

DESCRIPTION

Harbor seals (*Phoca vitulina*) are found in both the Atlantic and Pacific Oceans. Their coats are spotted and can range from a light gray to dark brown or black. The males, which are slightly larger than the females, can weigh as much as 300 pounds and reach 5-6 feet in length. Compared to the sea lion, the true seals have an internal ear, smaller front flippers, and no hinged hip joint. They seem to undulate across rocky shorelines although they are deceptively fast. They propel themselves along in the water with their rear flippers and steer with the front ones.

They can turn in a flash when chased by prey, such as a shark, or chasing fish, their primary food source, for dinner.

BEHAVIOR

During the daylight hours, harbor seals often haul out onto rocks or inlets of small islands and shores. They congregate in small groups or alone. Usually, an alert observer might spot the head of one or a pair as they swim along the coast. They are cautious and will quickly slip into the water if approached. However, as a protected species under the Marine Mammal Protection Act, they should not be disturbed. Stiff fines may be imposed up to $100,000 in some cases in the U.S. for disturbing marine mammals (see the link below for details). If an injury or sick animal is suspected, call the nearest public aquarium as these have the resources to respond to stranded animals regardless of the species. They are easily trained and, thus make a popular addition to many public aquariums and zoos.

https://www.leaguelaw.com/wp-content/uploads/2014/08/Distrubing%20Whales.pdf

REPRODUCTION

Harbor seals are known to be monogamous and mate in the water. The females are nurturing to their pups, which are typically born with whitish lanugo hair and able to swim shortly after birth. They become sexually mature around 5 years and mate in the summer and spring. Gestation is approximately 10 months with pups weighing about 25 pounds. The mother's milk is rich in fat, and they may nurse for up to 6 weeks while they remain in a nursery.

CONSERVATION

While the harbor seal population is robust, NOAA sites the following dangers for this species as, net entanglement, illegal feeding and harassment, habitat degradation, chemical contaminants, oil spills, energy exploration, vessel collisions, disturbance, and disease.

Resources:

https://www.fisheries.noaa.gov/species/harbor-seal

http://www.animalspot.net/harbor-seal.html

Grey (or Gray) seals

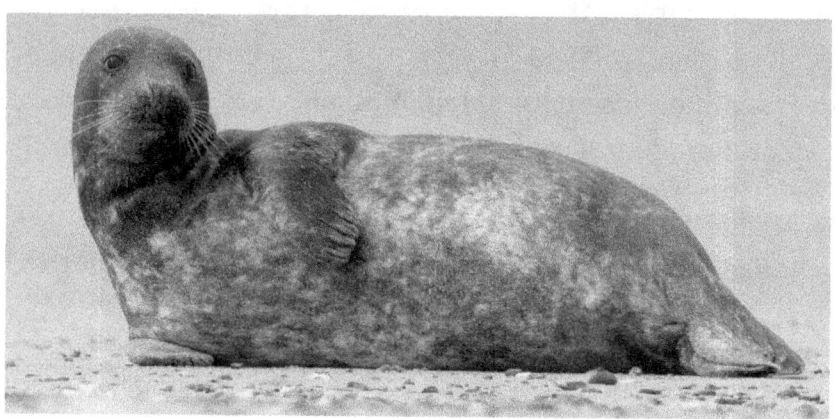

DESCRIPTION

Grey (or Gray) seals, (*Halichoerus grypus*), is also known as the horsehead head seal due to its distinctive elongated head and neck. The scientific name means "hooked-nose pig of the sea." The coloration is dark to light grey with the males larger than the females weighing up to 900 pounds. Like the harbor seal, they are "true" seals, lacking an external ear and a hinged hip joint. They, too, swim primarily with their rear flippers (although Woody, described in our story, adapted to the loss of his rear flippers due to frostbite shortly after birth). Their current range is the Atlantic coastline primarily in colder regions. They are a favorite target of great white sharks.

BEHAVIOR

Grey seals congregate in large rookeries, particularly during mating season. They are often spotted swimming at sea with only their head and neck visible and can dive to over 1000 feet while holding their breath for an hour. Like the harbor seal, they move like a caterpillar undulating across rocky areas or sandy beaches.

REPRODUCTION

Unlike the harbor seal, the males are not monogamous and will mate with several different females during the breeding season. Gestation is around 11 months, and they give birth to a single female. Mating occurs in early winter on the east coast of the United States. Nursing lasts about 3 months with the mother's milk extremely high in fat. They hunt in groups and can locate their prey even in murky waters with their excellent sense of echolocation.

CONSERVATION

According to NOAA's website, *"Gray seals can become entangled in fishing gear and other types of marine debris, either swimming off with the gear attached or becoming anchored. They can become entangled in many different gear types, including gillnets, trawls, purse seines, or weirs. Once entangled, seals may drown if they cannot reach the surface to breathe, or they may drag and swim with attached gear for long distances. This can ultimately result in fatigue, compromised feeding ability, or severe injury, which may lead to reduced reproductive success and death."*

NOAA also adds this warning: *"Gray seals are easy to view in the wild, but this puts them at higher risk of human-related injuries and death. Feeding (or trying to feed) them is harmful and illegal because it changes their natural behaviors and makes them less wary of people and vessels. They learn to associate humans with an easy meal and change their natural hunting practices — for example, they take bait catch directly off fishing gear. Sometimes they fall victim to retaliation (such as shooting) by frustrated boaters and fishermen.*

They may also be disturbed or harassed by the presence of humans and watercraft. Harassment is illegal and happens when any act of pursuit, torment, or annoyance might injure them or disrupt their behaviors. Remember to share the shore with gray seals for their safety and yours."

Grey seals are also subject to the same dangers as the harbor seal and are a favorite food of white sharks. It is dangerous to swim, snorkel, dive, surf, or boogie board near areas where Grey seals are present since inadvertent attacks on human may occur.

Resources:

https://www.fisheries.noaa.gov/species/gray-seal

Elephant seals

DESCRIPTION

The Northern elephant seal (*Mirounga angusterostris*) is the smaller of two species. The larger Southern elephant seal (*M. leonina*) is found in the Antarctic region while the northern species has colonies on the California coast and the Channel Islands off the coast of Alaska. The Southern species is some 40% larger than the quite large Northern species. The males can reach a weight of 400 pounds and a length of 13 feet.

A true seal (all of the characteristics), the elephant seal is easily distinguished by its inflatable proboscis most notably on the males. They are brown to dark gray in color and move by undulating like a caterpillar along the shores. The front flippers are almost prehensile and used to cover themselves with sand to keep cool on sandy beaches. The males can lift their bodies to a nearly erect position which intimidates other males as they compete for females during the breeding season in the rookeries.

BEHAVIOR

The Northern elephant seal spends significant time at sea diving at depths over 2500 feet and can stay submerged for 30 minutes or more. Males fight vigorously with one another to earn the right to mate with several females. Their diet is primarily squid and fish.

REPRODUCTION

Males establish harems and fight with competing younger males for the right to breed often with several of the females. The gestation is approximately 11 months with birthing in early winter. Breeding may take place while the pups are still dependent on their mothers, generally about a month.

CONSERVATION

NOAA reports that numbers are difficult to ascertain since this species spends little time on land. However, they site dangers for this species as: net entanglement, illegal feeding and harassment, habitat degradation, chemical contaminants, oil spills, energy exploration, vessel collisions, disturbance, and disease.

Resources:

https://www.fisheries.noaa.gov/species/northern-elephant-seal

Common Bottlenose Dolphin and Beluga Whale

Since there is a significant amount of information on these much-studied species, we will give a cursory discussion and provide some information about these animals' conservation.

The Bottlenose dolphin (*Tursiops truncatus*) gained popularity with a television show called "Flipper" back in 1964. Many dolphins were killed when caught in tuna nets until authorities stepped in. Tuna companies responded with a net maneuver allowing dolphins to escape and marked tuna cans "dolphin-free," to appease the buying public. Not all companies have complied to the strict rules involving the labeling as dolphin-free. For an update, see the following International Marine Mammal Project website:

http://savedolphins.eii.org/news/entry/saving-dolphins-from-tuna-nets-an-update

http://www.allaboutwildlife.com/dolphins-whales/the-disturbing-facts-about-dolphin-safe-tuna/4298

Additionally, The Marine Mammal Protection Agency lists 5 dolphin stocks as depleted:

- Western North Atlantic Central Florida Coastal stock

- Western North Atlantic Northern Florida Coastal stock

- Western North Atlantic Northern Migratory Coastal stock

- Western North Atlantic South Carolina-Georgia Coastal stock

- Western North Atlantic Southern Migratory Coastal stock

NOAA lists the following threats to the dolphin population: Entanglement, Illegal feeding and harassment, Habitat degradation, Noise, Chemical contaminants, Oil spills, and energy exploration, Disease, Biotoxins, and Vessel collisions. It has an extensive discussion on each of these topics at:

https://www.fisheries.noaa.gov/species/common-bottlenose-dolphin

https://www.fisheries.noaa.gov/species/common-bottlenose-dolphin

The Beluga whale (*Delphinapterus leucas*) is a member of the same Order as the bottlenose dolphin, *Cetacea*. It is found in the Arctic regions and Alaska. The beluga whale is easily recognizable by its distinctive and strikingly white coloration, and dome on top of its head called a melon. NOAA says of the population, *"Beluga whales are vulnerable to many stressors and threats, including pollution, habitat degradation, harassment, interactions with commercial and recreational fisheries, oil and gas exploration, disease, and other types of human disturbance such as underwater noise."*

Some areas have been depleted of stock and numbers are declining with the current status as "Near Threatened" by the ICUN. Many public aquariums are involved in conservation efforts through scientific research and promoting public awareness of this beautiful creature with the likable face.

Resources:

https://www.bioexpedition.com/beluga-whale/

https://www.mysticaquarium.org/2017/02/21/beluga-whale-research-continues-at-mystic-aquarium/

https://www.fisheries.noaa.gov/feature-story/potential-impacts-noise-endangered-beluga-whales-cook-inlet

https://www.afsc.noaa.gov/Science_blog/Cook_Inlet_acoustic_monitoring_main.htm

Lionfish

The lionfish (*Pterois volitans*), once inhabited only the Indian and South Pacific oceans. However, sometime during the 1980s, they began appearing more frequently in the waters off Florida, possibly as a consequence of aquarium enthusiasts releasing them as unwanted "pets." A voracious eater with poisonous spines, they grew at an alarming pace with no real predators. Thus, the eloquent fish with flowing fins and spectacular orange, black and red coloration, became one of the premier examples of an invasive species — that is, an animal (or plant) not indigenous to a region.

Several efforts to thwart the proliferation of the lionfish invasion have had a measure of success, but the numbers continue to increase exponentially. The flesh of the lionfish, although safe to eat despite the poisonous spines, fails to entice consumers for fear of ciguatera. Ciguatera is described as follows by eMedicine Health as follows, *"Symptoms include nausea, vomiting, diarrhea, muscle pain, numbness, tingling, abdominal pain, dizziness, and vertigo. The classic finding of hot and cold sensation reversal is actually a burning sensation on contact with cold (allodynia). Severe cases of ciguatera poisoning may result in shortness of breath, salivation, tearing, chills, rashes, itching, and paralysis. Bradycardia, coma, and hypotension can occur. Death due to poisoning is rare (less than 0.5 %)."* Little wonder that the lionfish tend to lack appeal even though not a single case of ciguatera poisoning has been reported. Of course, caution is recommended when preparing the fish as the spine is sharp. While removing it along with the poison glands, there is the potential of receiving a painful sting.

Culling has thus far been unsuccessful. One group offers a T-shirt to the first 250 fishermen to catch the fish. However, NOAA comments, *"Most scientists agree, it is unlikely that the lionfish's invasion of U.S. waters can be reversed. Any large-scale attempts to remove the existing lionfish from U.S. Atlantic waters appear impractical and would be very costly, because of the large geographic range and depths that the fish now occupies."*

Dire predictions are that the lionfish will quickly decimate smaller indigenous species of fish and impact the delicate coral reef systems already overtaxed by other threats such as warming of the oceans, sedimentation, and damage from divers and snorkelers, to name a few. Time will tell if these predictions will come true or if some local predators will adapt and balance out the invasion. The outlook is not hopeful, however.

Resources:

https://oceana.org/blog/invasive-lionfish-are-delicious-—-it-safe-eat-them-6

https://www.theonlinefisherman.com/conservation/methods-to-reduce-lionfish-population-assessed

https://oceanservice.noaa.gov/education/stories/lionfish/lion05_stop.html

Photo and illustration credits

Pg	Photo/Illus	Author	Adobe® License#
Cover		LifeGemz	196043465
3	cunner	unknown	
4	flounder	en.wicktionary.org	
4	sandworm	Alexander Semenov	
10	New London Day	Skip Wiesenberger	
11	Author		
13	Author		
14	Sea lion	Patrick Rolands	86663944
16	Harbor seal	ksumano	96167718
21	Grey seal	davehuntphoto	46763863
27	Man-o-war	7activestudio	70379888
31	Lionfish	Sergey Skleznev	20410317
48	Sand tiger	Ruslan Gilmanshin	98055834
67	Jawfish	John Anderson	9234054
68	Lemon shark	Wikipedia/Albert Kok	
69	Grey seal pup	Andrea Izzotti	130240778
81	Elephant seal	Sergey Rusakov	183100076
82	Elephant seal	andymorehouse	97082820
89	Sea lion	Xaver Klaussner	136585308
94	Dolphins	IgorZh	55159208
103	Dolphin	agno-agnus	1849156
108	Beluga whale	SeanPavone	35363579
133	Blue shark		
138	Shark Tank	www.NorwalkAquarium.org	
145	Harbor seal	randimal	72344017
148	Grey seal	Artush Foto	107741861

This is page Addendum

www.ingramcontent.com/pod-product-compliance
Lightning Source LLC
Chambersburg PA
CBHW072048280526
45788CB00006B/2232